Hope For Survival

Peter N Muya

Published by BISHOP PETER N MUYA.

HOPE FOR SURVIVAL

Peter N Muya

First edition. July 2024.

Second edition. May 2025

For information contact Bishop Peter Muya via muyabishop@gmail.com or via phone +254724805868/+254798649468

Edited by Peter Hinga Kiago. Email: quibpet3r@gmail.com phone +254706488565

I dedicate this book to wife Mary Gathoni and our children, Nyambura, Faith and Muya. I do thank the lord for their support in my ministry and I trust that each one of them will know the lords enabling, encouragement and blessing as they continue to bring up their children in God's way. I keep on upholding them with my prayers in their lives and ministries.

I also dedicate it to my lovely grandsons and granddaughters.

CHAPTER ONE

THE WAY OF PEACE WITH GOD

We live in a world contaminated by sin. Sin is anything that goes against God's holy standards. When we don't follow the scripture, we are guilty of sin. Sin separates us from God, the source of life.

Since the first man and woman, Adam and Eve, sinned in the Garden of Eden, sin has been universal. The Bible says that "all have sinned and come short of the glory of God" (*Romans 3:23 KJV*). It also says the natural consequence for sin is eternal death, or punishment in an eternal hell. The Bible says, "Then when lust hath conceived, it bringeth forth sin; and sin, when it is finished, bringeth forth death" (*James 1:15*).

One day, God gave me a twofold vision. Firstly, it's reaching the unreached, and secondly, it's giving hope to the hopeless, hurting world.

This book is about our second objective in the ministry, giving hope to the hopeless in this hurting world.

When we look around our communities in Africa, what do we see? There so many refugees, the hopeless, homeless, the poor, the hungry, and the sick. HIV/AIDS and war are the most common emerging issues in our communities in Africa.

As a minister of the gospel, I'm asking all ministers of the gospel to come out of their comfort zones and go out to serve and meet people's needs. Let us be merciful and compassionate. Let us give our bodies as living sacrifices to help others in this hurting world.

In today's fast-paced society, we are always searching for new ways to handle stress in the lives of orphans, widows, people living with HIV/AIDS, refugees, and the hurting.

Many authors have written books on stress, and psychologists are offering endless advice on how to get out of it. But the experts working with us in the outreach programs of our ministry have all agreed that the key to handling the everyday stress in our lives is by having inner peace, which is only found in Jesus Christ.

I have ministered to stressed people, even victims of HIV/ AIDS, and I have encouraged them to receive Jesus Christ as their savior. Many are being transformed, delivered, and healed.

The only way to handle stress is by receiving the inner peace that comes by accepting Jesus Christ, the Prince of Peace. Many widows, orphans, HIV/AIDS victims, drug addicts, and other hurting people are being delivered from stress related problems after receiving Jesus Christ in their souls. We encourage victims to live spiritual lives so that they cannot be trapped by the snares of stress or depression.

I am ministering these life changing messages to help all those with stress related problems. If you are suffering from any of these problems, please let us know.

For the youth, we have a program in our church to help them in their economic and social development. We introduce them to the digital world by assisting them in networking through the internet, where they can use computer skills and other essential skills to make money. Through this program, we help to eradicate poverty, joblessness, hopelessness, idleness, drug abuse, and HIV/AIDS transmission. We have counseling sessions on entrepreneurship ventures and other social problems affecting the youth.

I have written books to help in our outreach programs, namely: "Do Not Weep," "I Shall Not Die," "Kill Me Not" "Never Lose Hope" and "Love Without Lust". In this chaotic and hurting world, Jesus Christ is the Prince of Peace.

What is more tiresome than a dark night when you are not feeling well, and you cannot sleep? That night the hours pass by slowly. At last, you see the first sunbeams of the morning. The birds begin to sing, and everything seems to brighten.

The state of the world before Jesus came was like a dark night. Israel's prophet wrote that people walked in darkness. The wonderful light of God's Son would brighten the dark and sinful world.

For a long time, nobody knew just when or where the Savior would be born. After many years, the prophecies about the birth of a savior were forgotten. There was no message from heaven for four hundred years. But God knew just the right time to fulfill all the prophecies corning the birth of the Savior.

God sent the angel Gabriel to the earth with a message of peace and hope to a virgin called Mary. Gabriel knew the city and the village in which she was living. He went straight to Mary and said to her, "Rejoice, highly favored [one], the Lord [is] with you; blessed [are] you among women!" (*Luke 1:28 NKJV*).

Mary was very frightened by the voice of God, but the angel encouraged her, saying, "Do not be afraid Mary...you are going to have a son. He will be very special. He will be called the son of the Highest...whose kingdom will last forever" (*Luke 1:30–33*). Mary asked the angel, "But how can this happen? I am a virgin" (*Luke 1:34*).

Gabriel answered, "The Holy Spirit will come upon you, and God's power will rest on you. That is why your child will be in you. That is why your child will be God's own son. Nothing is too hard to God" (*Luke 1:35*).

After this message, Mary was married to Joseph to fulfill what the angel had told her, and in the fullness of time, Jesus was born in Bethlehem. They both called the baby "Jesus," just as the angel had said.

The good news about the birth of Jesus was communicated to the wise men, who were led by a star to where Jesus was wrapped in a manger. They give Him gifts and worshiped Him.

Jesus grew up, and after becoming twenty years old, He started teaching in the church. A time came when He called the twelve disciples, and they followed Him. Later, He told them that He would be killed by evil men, but on the third day, He would rise again from the dead. The disciples did not understand these things until they happened.

Jesus was taken to Pilate to be judged before He was killed. Pilate did not want to condemn an innocent man, but the angry mob kept on roaring, "Crucify Him! Crucify Him!" Soon, they began to shout, "Set Barabbas free."

Nervously, Pilate washed his hands before the crowd. He said, "I am not responsible for the death of this righteous man" (*Matthew 27:24 GNT*). He tried to save Jesus, but the mob would not allow him. The evil soldiers whipped Jesus severely, and then they forced a crown of thorns on His head, dressed Him in a purple robe, and placed a stick (a mock scepter) in His right hand. The mob kept on shouting, "Crucify Him! Crucify Him!"

They nailed His hands and feet to the cross in the middle of two thieves. They pierced His ribs with a spear. Jesus was in great agony and died on the cross. At noon, the whole world was plunged into darkness. Jesus kept on suffering for three more lonely hours, but before He died, He gave a shout of victory when He declared, "It is finished!" (*John 19:30 NKJV*).

His work on earth was done. Suddenly, the earth shook, rocks split, and many graves were opened. The frightened soldiers exclaimed, "Surely this was the son of God!" (*Matthew 27:54*).

Jesus' faithful friends watched the crucifixion from a distance. It was heartbreaking to watch their beloved savior die. On the third day, as He had said, very early in the morning, a great earthquake shook the tomb. A blinding light flashed on the sleepy soldiers standing on guard. It was an angel from heaven, with a face like lightning and a robe as white as snow. The terror stricken guards shook like leaves before him, completely helpless. In power and great glory, Jesus rose from the dead. The angel rolled the huge stone away from the entrance and sat on it.

Meanwhile, Mary Magdalene, Mary (the mother of James), and other women were coming towards the tomb. They were frightened when they saw the angel. But he said kindly, "Do not fear, I know you are looking for Jesus who was crucified. He is not here, for He has risen…Go quickly and tell His disciples" (*Matthew 28:5–7 NASB*).

The women fled from the tomb, trembling and speechless—their hearts filled with fear and great joy. Jesus died for us; He carried our sins, our iniquities, our death, our sorrow, and our grief. He delivered us from the eternal death in hell.

The Bible says, "For God so loved the world that He gave His only begotten Son, that whosoever believes in Him should not perish but have everlasting life" (*John 3:16 KJV*).

We are born again through the power of the Holy Spirit and develop new desires and attitudes (*2 Corinthians 5:17*). We begin to make the right choices for our hearts to have peace with God. Our hearts are changed as we continue growing in grace day by day. Jesus assured his followers, "Peace I leave with you, my peace I give you; not as the world gives do I give you. Let not your hearts be troubled, neither let it be afraid" (*John 14:27*).

The Bible gives us the way of peace with God. "Therefore, having been justified by faith, we have peace with God through our Lord Jesus Christ" (*Romans 5:1 NKJV*). Verse two says, "Through whom also we have access by faith into this grace in which we stand, and rejoice in the hope of the glory of God" (*Romans 5:2*).

Since the day I received Jesus Christ as my personal savior, over forty years ago, I have been preaching the messages of peace, hope, love, and faith in this hurting world.

In my life and ministry, I have experienced many trials and tragedies, but God has brought me through all of them. I believe that with Jesus Christ in my soul, I am what God says I am. I can do what God says I can do. In the word of God, all my questions in life are answered.

This confidence assures and enables me to remain calm and in peace through all circumstances in life. I have stability in Jesus Christ, and inner peace, which holds me up when life threatens to overwhelm me.

I will keep on swinging at life's trials as I serve my God in all circumstances in this hurting world. Today, I am busy reaching the unreached and giving hope to the hopeless in this chaotic world. My hope is in God. "Now faith is the substance of the things hoped for, the evidence of things not seen" (*Hebrews 11:1*). Hope is a very powerful means of strengthening me in prayer. I pray with great hope that God will hear prayer. My hope is fixed upon God's word. Hope is the anchor of my faith that God is faithful to fulfill these promises, and that He will not alter the things He has spoken with His mouth. I am diligent in prayer; therefore, I will never be destitute of hope. The word of God encourages me. "Whatsoever things were written aforetime was written for our learning, that we through patience and comfort of the Scriptures might have hope" (*Romans 15:4*).

There is no time in life where I will stop hoping in God. Hope in God is more potent than mere wishful thinking, and it is more active than longing. It is the desire with an earnest expectation of fulfillment. "But as for me, I will hope continually and will praise thee yet more and more" (*Psalm 71:14 DBT*).

I hope for the second coming of Jesus Christ. He is my constant inspiration. This hope is cheering me on to continue during lonely or hard times. It makes me preach the Word as never before.

The whole world is looking for this inner peace, but without Jesus in their souls, they will never get it. Recently the world leaders held a global peace forum in Geneva, Switzerland. The main agenda of this global forum was peace and security. All world leaders tried to tackle various challenges facing the world today.

Among the various global security challenges, terrorism stood out as one of the most sophisticated and challenging issues to handle. Terrorism is a human imposed disaster aimed at maximizing mass destruction through the use of violent action to achieve a political agenda.

Everywhere in the world, nations are crying for peace: in countries, cities, towns, villages, schools, colleges, and homes. World leaders are making strategies that can be used internationally to end terrorism, which is a great threat to world peace. Terrorism, with all its manifestation and activities, violates human rights. It is one of the prophetic signs of the coming of Jesus Christ on the earth again.

Our loving Creator has given the world a clear way of escaping the coming judgment and the way of receiving inner peace through receiving Jesus Christ, the Redeemer, Savior, and the Prince of Peace in this world.

Sin has made people believe the lies of the devil, and they are left confused and overwhelmed with fear without peace of mind in their lives. We can all agree that the world is in a more chaotic condition than at any previous time. Yet, our leaders have tried to find solutions through peace forums, world cooperation's, and treaties, but the result is chaos and more chaos. For example, recently, Kenya experienced mass destruction when the terrorists rained down fire from bombs and guns, causing deaths in Nairobi, Mombasa, and Garissa.

As I write, our armed forces are risking their lives on foreign land to keep us safe from these terrorists. Our peace is being defended on the battlefield in Somalia by our selfless armed forces.

More than anything else, these attacks should remind us that Christians should pray for our nation, Kenya. I believe that true peace comes from Almighty God through the prayers and fasting of all believers. Jesus is the Prince of Peace.

Although wars and turmoil seem to be raging around our borders, we find peace and refuge through prayers to our Lord Jesus Christ. He encourages us to "pursue peace with all people, and holiness, without which no one will see the Lord" (*Hebrews 12:14*).

If we earnestly present our request to Jesus Christ through prayers and humble ourselves before Him, He will answer our prayers in all ways, and peace will reign in our troubled hearts.

This book will help you on how to find the real, living, and everlasting peace in your hurting soul by receiving the Prince of Peace. Jesus is the same yesterday, today, and forever.

CHAPTER TWO

AFRICA BELONGS TO GOD

In 1985, when I was in a season of prayer and fasting, God revealed to me a wonderful, soul thrilling vision. I saw the Lord God in His beautiful throne in Heaven. It was a splendid, majestic, magnificent vision. As I looked at the sight fixedly, I was utterly awestruck. I encountered the radiance of His great glory in His presence. This was a direct encounter with El-Shaddai, the great provider in my life.

Before me, there was a beautiful picture of the continent of Africa, shaped like a question mark. In the picture, I saw millions of different black people from many different nations in Africa. Many people were suffering, crying, while others were mourning for the deaths of their loved ones. People were living with great pain in their lives from different kinds of calamities: tragedies, disasters, diseases, famines, floods, and other social, physical, or economic crises. Because of the increasing spread of deadly diseases such as HIV/AIDS, millions of people were dying daily without hope.

As I looked in horror, a voice said, "I have called you to reach the unreached in Africa!" Suddenly, I woke up with a stirring memory of this awesome vision God had given me. A vision of "reaching the unreached in Africa!"

God spoke to me in the vision very clearly, just as He had spoken to His servant Moses in the burning bush. The voice of God was calling me into the ministry with an irresistible divine force. I thanked God. I was called for a divine mission, and I knew that the gifts and the calling of God are irrevocable (Romans 11:29).

God gave me a lifesaving vision. My mission was to reach and win the lost, the needy, the oppressed, and the captives. I was called to give hope to the hopeless, the AIDS orphans, widows, street children, the destitute, and the less fortunate. My divine mandate was to win souls for Christ, before it was too late. Since the day God gave me this vision, I have carried a great burden for Africa in my life. Africa is in my heart, and the ends of the earth in my mind.

I have been winning souls in every part of our country for the past twenty years. I have been preaching Christ before crowds of thousands in towns, villages, cities, parks, slums, ghettos, schools, colleges, armed forces, police stations, bus stations, hotels, restaurants, coffee bars in the streets, in the open air, and town halls. With my whole being, I have been echoing the cry everywhere— "Africa belongs to Jesus!"

I have been going out to the most remote areas to reach the unreached. I have met with some needy people who told me that no one has ever told them of the gospel and that there was not any church available in their area. I have a great challenge before me. I am face-to-face with the command of Jesus, "Go ye therefore and make disciples of all nations" (Matthew 28: 19). My spirit has developed a burning passion for souls—what an overwhelming experience in the ministry. My ministry is to preach the word in season and out of season (2 Timothy 4:2).

As I write, I'm busy in my pastorate in Nairobi, the international coordination office of Gospel Messengers

Fellowship. I also have a full diary of preaching the Word in many other places in our country. I can say that "truly my soul waiteth upon God: from him cometh my salvation...He is my defense; I shall not be greatly moved (Psalm 62:1–2 KJV).

I am guided in my decision-making by four key components: vision, ministry, motto, and prayer. I am a full-time pastor of Gospel Messengers Fellowship, a ministry that unites all other gospel messengers from all corners of the world. But we are emphasizing reaching Africa first. We are many gospel messengers united in the spirit of love, ministry, vision, call, and brotherhood. We are willing to support anybody willing to take forth the Great Commission to all parts of the world, regardless of sex, color, race or culture.

I thank God for His faithfulness in confirming my vision through His servant and renowned world apostle and prophet, Dr. Morris Cerullo. When this man of God visited Kenya in April 1999, he spoke a prophetic utterance to the body of Christ in Africa. He said, "God is going to raise Africans; they will not reach Africa only, but the whole world. I prophesy that every country in Africa will be opened to the gospel. "He ended the message by saying, "Africa needs breakthroughs. One thing God told me to tell you is that you are going to get financial breakthroughs."

I have proven that "surely God does nothing, Unless He reveals His secrets to his servants the prophets "(Amos.3: 7 NKJV).

So I received the message in my spirit because I believed that it came straight from heaven. Africa indeed belongs to Jesus. I believed that I'm one in God's victorious army. I remember the words the Lord told Dr. Cerullo in Africa in

1962 when He told him, "Son, build me an army." Today we have millions of God's army in the whole world that God uses in many beautiful ways to do His works.

The power of God was evident in my life and ministry. The anointing was very profound and rooted deeply in my ministry because of the confirmation of my vision. I had a new power in my life that could not be defeated by the enemy's power, ever again. God miraculously answered my prayer. I believe the words of the prophet of God, "Believe in the LORD your God and you will be established; believe His prophets, and you will prosper" (2 Chronicles 20:20).

My vision is two-fold: firstly, it is to reach the unreached; secondly, it is to give hope to the hopeless, the AIDS victims, the widows, the destitute, and the less fortunate in AFRICA. It gives me great pleasure in serving the needy. As the body of Christ, we are coming together in fellowship, and we are renewing our commitment to serve our Lord in various responsibilities in the ministry. In Africa, we have been experiencing people being killed and property destroyed in tribal clashes. God has given me a burden to reflect on all these issues that are affecting many people and causing many untimely deaths.

I am called as a messenger of hope to bring the greatest spiritual awakening and renewal in Africa. My spirit calls for Africa to "Awake! Arise! And Shine! For your light has come!" The only way that this wonderful revival and healing can come to Africa is through Jesus Christ. It is my sincere hope that all people in Africa are willing to live by faith in Christ so that He can bring light to this modern, although distressed, society. With God, all things are possible.

How could I, as village gospel messenger, achieve my ambition's dream of giving hope to the hopeless in Africa?

With a few committed believers, I started, Stay Up Rehabilitative Community Based Organization, a community based project to minister to the hopeless around us. We minister to all those who are bound by alcohol, sex, drug addiction, and violent crimes. This is a community based organization (CBO) in Kiambogo Village, Gilgil Division.

We are in a rehabilitation business. Because we are living in terrible times when HIV/AIDS is one of the greatest threats to the people of Africa, our ministry had to redefine our mission statement and our vision to make the gospel more relevant and acceptable to the rapidly changing society. Africa needs a new breed of committed spiritual leaders who will give our continent a new hope and a new direction.

In this regard, we are focusing on our vision of reaching the unreached and giving the hopeless hope to face the future with confidence. Our mission in this hurting continent is to be agents of hope and reconciliation. This project that began locally is now acting globally. We are willing to serve and support the community in any way possible, be it through prayer or sharing of our resources.

The objectives of the project

1. To take people to a new level of victory where everybody will be 100 percent whole in spirit, soul, and body. The word of God says, "For I will restore health to you and heal you of your wounds, says the LORD" (Jeremiah 30: 17).
2. To give hope to the hopeless, the AIDS orphans, widows, street children, the destitute, and the less fortunate.
3. To give medical care services to the community through mobile clinics. We take care of the sick and the afflicted in their own homes. We have a heart full of hope and love for those infected and afflicted by
HIV/AIDS. We help to reduce the risk of HIV/ AIDS transmission by promoting family and community awareness of HIV/ AIDS prevention and care and giving spiritual and pastoral care counseling to hundreds of people who are struggling with the illness and the disability that come with AIDS.

WE HAVE MILLIONS OF AIDS orphans facing an uncertain future, with no basic necessities of survival and with no parental guidance. They need all our care and compassion. Many people in Africa are struggling and suffering from civil strife and conflicts. Others are suffering from famines, physical abuse, especially sexual abuse. In our cities, we have an increase of violent crimes due to idleness and unemployment.

Everywhere in Africa, people are crying. You can hear the cry of the hopeless, the AIDS orphans, the widows, the destitute street children, and the less fortunate. People are crying because they cannot achieve their expectations in life. Millions of people are suffering from depression and stress because of the many problems in their lives. I have personally met desperate people who have reached the point of wishing to be allowed to die to escape their problems.

Many people lay their heads on their pillows at night without being sure of their destiny. They have much anxiety over being sure of the fate of their souls. Others have so much anxiety about the next day that they would prefer to die before they wake. Many people have many family problems, emotional struggles, or employment difficulties, making them wish it would better to be taken out of this life before the morning sun rises, and before facing another agonizing day.

In my twenty years of ministry, I have seen many desperate people coming to the place where they felt there was no way out. They want to die by committing suicide. They find the world to be crumbling around them. They are unable to bear it anymore. They have drifted apart and can't carry it anymore. They are so physically and emotionally exhausted that they want to take their own lives.

I have experienced that most people who take their own lives do so when they are deeply depressed. Reality becomes distorted, so they can't see the selfish and sinful nature of their evil actions. It's important to note that the causes of depression are differing. In some common causes, I've noticed that depression is caused by calamity after calamity, and the victims become unable to cope with their terrible problems and situations. I have seen many people who are depressed by being overwhelmed by the powers of witchcraft. They are afflicted in their minds, spirits, and emotions. They cry in the darkness, not knowing the way of deliverance. They live with an inner cry in their soul that can lead them to breakdown or heart attack.

As a gospel messenger of hope, I am ministering to these people who are unable to cope with others, for they think that everybody is against them. Through our project, we are willing to restore and uphold them. Sometimes we speak hope directly to their souls. We use sensitive ways of caring for these people: a word, a smile, and a helping hand. To all those who are cast down, in Christ there is hope.

We speak hope to people when they are ready to perish. God is ready to restore and save people. By placing their trust in Christ, people can now close their eyes at night with the assurance that their problems of tomorrow will not be greater than the living Christ in their souls. After people come to Jesus, they can fall asleep with confidence that God cares for their lives. People have certainty that whether they awake or die before they wake, they are in God's divine protection.

We tell people to trust in God to keep out despair! We ask them to remind themselves of God's goodness and love. We talk to them directly about their needs. We help them find new hope beyond the failures of life that causes them to despair. Their new hope is born in their hearts because God is alive. No one is hopeless whose hope is in God. He is their hope when the situation is hopeless.

When our expectation is rooted in God and His Son, Jesus Christ, as our savior from sin and death, the blessings promised in His word becomes a reality in our lives. Because our God is within us, there is hope. He always keeps hope flowing even when the spring dried up in human life. The secret of coping is hoping in God. This helps us face what lies ahead of us, Africa. The Bible says, "They shall neither hunger anymore nor thirst anymore; the sun shall not strike them, nor any heat...God will wipe away every tear from their eyes" (Revelation 7:16–17).

The thing that I know about my future is that God meets my needs before dawn as I face what lies ahead. I hope in God for tomorrow's provision, even in the darkest times in my life. In Africa, I have the brightest hope in God. That's why I started the project in our ministry to minister love and hope to the hopeless. People who worry about stress and anxiety do not realize these are an integral part of their condition. Truly in Africa, depression is a severe and unrecognized problem, and many people who are suffering from it are misunderstood and mishandled.

I have seen that victims of depression feel inferior. They lose self-respect, self-worth, and hope for change. Because we are messengers of hope, we are healing the troubled souls in Africa. We are ministering to the hurting by caring for their needs so that the causes of harm in their lives can be eradicated in society. God has called us to make a difference in this hurting world.

I thank God for giving us a dream of establishing a project to serve the community around us, and as we serve needy people through God's love, we can see the fruits. We have seen many people coming to Christ as we share the gospel and give them our testimonies. We have sacrificially invested ourselves in serving others in love. We are touching many hurting souls by loving the unloved.

Sometimes serving the needy can be adventurous until the end. But we are always ready to face each adventure in the project. It is very important to note that we started our project in the remote village Kiambogo, Elementaita, where there are no electricity or telephone services, and where the road network is very poor, making transport very inconvenient.

The village is in a lovely area where you could enjoy every type of traditionally cooked meals, and it has all you could expect in an African village. During the rainy season, the roads are impassable, and people are forced to treat their sick at home through traditional and local remedies.

Eventually, during the rainy season, most sick people die before they get to the nearest health center due to poor roads. The health center that is near our home is about seven kilometers away, and every time you visit, the doctors disappoint you by telling you that there is no medicine.

Our project has been receiving support from some American missionaries, Ken and Sandy Taylor. They have been visiting our village very regularly with their mobile clinics. They have been using their four-wheel vehicle during the rainy season to bring health services in the community. After serving the sick, we take them to our home where they can enjoy our African meals and relax in the bed at night.

In the morning, we take them for a short walk around the village where they meet with children, men, and women before going to serve the sick in the clinic. On Sunday, we take them to the village church, where they enjoy our African ways of worship. We praise the Lord with loud shouts, clapping, dancing, and beating of the drums. After the service, we bid them farewell until the next visit.

Our project has been featured very strongly in the rural area, and we have said that we shall never be silent while fatal diseases, such as HIV/AIDS, kill our brothers and sisters. We are preaching a holistic gospel—body, soul, and mind. Our fight with HIV/AIDS is a life-and-death battle. We are the army of God to fight this deadly disease that is killing millions of people every year. In the name of Jesus, we've been given the power to destroy all the works of the devil.

We are taking an aggressive attack on HIV/AIDS. We must remove the-holier-than-thou attitude and realize that Jesus had compassion for the sick. He touched and healed the lepers. Jesus saved and healed all types of diseases. That's why we are prepared to fight AIDS from the pulpit, as we declare war against all demons that cause this disease.

We are playing our role in AIDS prevention, and we are giving open public addresses on the risky ways of contracting the disease. We are working together with the government, and the NGOs are supplementing our resources so that we can continue to play a role in fostering sound moral and religious values to fight these deadly diseases.

We don't care about risking our lives by going into the most dangerous places, like the slums and ghettos, where the drug addicts, prostitutes, and violent criminals live. We are called to minister God's love to the needy. We are to demonstrate Christ's practical love by going out there where the hurting souls are. We are to go out there where many people live and die without any church background.

But we share the gospel and totally quench the hidden thirst in their souls. We are reaching out in love. We connect hopeless people with big problems in their lives with Jesus, Who died and rose again for sinners. We are a small church that obeys the vision of God. We have a big vision.

That's why we are exploring the potential of establishing an international ministry's website, which will help us to network with our partners, churches, ministries, donor agencies, CBOs, NGOs, sponsors, support groups, health and social institutions.

We accept support from anybody or any other relevant agencies according to the needs of our project. We are providing coordination training in our ministry to advocate for the rights of the needy. Our network will involve sharing and seeking information from other people or organizations and working together in love. Our members can share our mission statement and help us with fundraising for our project.

We are looking for willing people who can help us network this vital ministry. We are creating a channel in our office in Nairobi for sharing resources, information, and ideas. If you are willing to assist us in any way, do let us know. We are eager to place your help where it is most needed. We are working together with volunteers, coordinators, and missionaries willing to work with us in the mission field. We are looking for people who are willing to work with us in an honoring capacity, without looking for money or any other material benefits. Our goal is to promote the social, physical, and spiritual conditions of the people in Africa.

God said, "Look, I am sending my messenger ahead of you, and he will prepare your way" Mark 1:2 NLT). My response is: "Send me, Lord, out where the sinners are." It has cost me a lot to be a gospel messenger. I have experienced persecution and many afflictions in my life. I have been opposed, ridiculed, beaten, and taken to the police because of preaching the gospel. But I have been preaching the gospel in and out of season. Even today, I preach without fear of the perils around me. I thank God for His protection in my life and ministry. He has given me Joshua's courage. I will preach, no matter the cost.

Since the day I accepted Jesus Christ as my personal savior, God has been doing great and wonderful things for me. Because of what He has been doing for other believers and for me, I have made a lasting decision to serve Him in all the days of my life. After many years of serving and trusting Him, I have experienced His power, anointing, blessing, glory, and His presence.

CHAPTER THREE

A MESSENGER OF HOPE

When God called me into the ministry, I had a deep love for souls, and it was my heart's desire to see souls saved. I preach Christ because He came into the world for only one purpose— to save the lost. I was always preaching "'not by might nor by power, but by My Spirit' says the LORD of hosts" (Zechariah 4:6).

I was sent to win souls for Christ, and I was only satisfied when I saw souls saved in my ministry. I trained Christians to be soul winners. I could not sit down in my little church or with my family and enjoy the comforts of life. I fulfilled the word of God, which says, "'You shall love your LORD your God with all of your heart, with all your soul, with all your mind, and with all your strength.' This is the first commandment" (Mark 12:30).

I was always preaching and waiting patiently like a fisherman waits for the fish to bite. I was always obedient to the vision of God in my life. God called me into the ministry as He called Moses in the burning bush. I heard His voice very clearly. His voice in my heart has an irresistible divine power. I was given a divine ministry. God's calling is irrevocable (Romans 11:29).

I was given a lifesaving ministry. I was a preacher of hope to the hopeless, the sick, the needy, the oppressed, and the less fortunate in life. I had a great burden for souls in Africa. Africa was in my heart and the ends of the earth in my mind. I have been preaching Christ in our country before crowds of people in towns, cities, villages, schools, colleges, slums, ghettos, hotels, and the open air.

Deep in my heart, I declared, "Africa belongs to Christ." I have been going to the remote areas to reach the unreached. I have gone to areas where the local people had no church. God's love consumed me, and I developed a burning desire to win souls for Christ. I could preach Christ in season and out of season.

As I write, I am swamped in my pastorate in Nairobi, one of the international coordination offices of the Gospel Messengers Fellowship. I have a full schedule of preaching Christ in many other towns and cities in the country. I'm an evangelist.

God guides me in my ministry. Our ministry unites all other gospel messengers from all corners of the world. We are emphasizing reaching Africa with the gospel of Christ. We are many united gospel messengers in one spirit of love, vision, call, and brotherhood.

I am a soul winner because Jesus said, "Go into all the world and preach the gospel to every creature" (Mark 16:15). This is a commission to the followers of Jesus Christ. This is my divine calling in the ministry. God's love overflows in my heart, and I preach Christ.

I am privileged to preach the gospel to every creature. This is my guarantee of happiness in my life. This is what I was called to do. I witness from house-to-house, in the markets, villages, on the busy streets, and everywhere.

I understand my calling out where the sinners are. Many Christians go in the church, but only a few who go out and witness to others. I am a soul winner—a witness and preacher of the gospel. The Great Commission is the reason behind my ministry.

My divine mandate is "to win souls."

My motto is "I shall not die but live and declare the works of the Lord." That's why I reach the unreached.

I love to share the gospel with the lost by every possible means. I use my voice to preach the gospel. I use channels of mass media and all other ways to reach the unreached. I have invested in the Great Commission.

I have been preaching in the crusades and face-to-face with hundreds of people. I am a gospel messenger. God has ordained me to preach the gospel. He speaks to sinners through me. He heals the brokenhearted and binds the wounds of the suffering. Christ's ministry in my community is expressed through me. I am the mouthpiece of God.

The Holy Spirit is working through my lips when I witness. I give the messages of hope and love to the needy. I am the temple of the Holy Spirit. Christ's love and mercy are manifested through me. Some people may never see Christ without me. God does not live in the church building; He lives in me to meet the needs of His people.

Let me tell you that you personally can be a gospel messenger abroad, even though you could never go abroad yourself.

You can invest in this ministry of reaching the unreached by giving any gift. Your gift could support a missionary in the mission field. You can sponsor a missionary.

Have you ever invested in the mission field? Start now, and you will have the joy of soul winning. Our top priority is soul winning. Every Christian is a soul winner; you and I are called to preach the gospel to the lost. We are ambassadors of Christ. Soul winning is God's heartbeat. Let us support one another in the ministry. We are willing to help anybody who is willing to take forth the Great

Commission to all parts of the world, regardless of sex, color, race, or culture.

We are very active in organizing crusades and open-air meetings. I write and print simple gospel tracts and distribute them to schools and colleges. We give books to distribute to the lost.

We have been giving hope to the victims of tribal clashes. God has given us a burden to reflect on all those who are suffering. I am calling Africa to "Awake! Arise! And Shine! for your light has come!" We believe we will see the greatest outpouring of the Holy Spirit in Africa.

As a full-time preacher, I cannot compromise the message of the cross, because I could perish. I have chosen to preach Christ, and Him crucified, without compromise. I do not want Christ to take my lamp stand and remove it from its place (Read Revelation 2:5).

As a village gospel messenger, I want to achieve my ambitions and dream of giving hope to the hopeless. I am ministering to all sinners who bound by alcohol, sex abuse, drug addiction, and crime. I am in a rehabilitation business.

We are living in terrible times when HIV/AIDS in the most significant threat in Africa. Our ministry is redefining our mission statement and vision to make the gospel more relevant and acceptable to the rapidly changing society. Africa needs a new breed of committed preachers who will preach Christ in this continent. Preachers who will give people hope and direction in their lives.

That's why we are focusing on our vision of reaching the unreached. We are giving the hopeless hope in this hurting world. We are agents of hope and reconciliation in his world. We are taking the needy to a new level of victory where they can receive healing of the spirit, soul, and body.

The word of God says, "For I will restore health to you, and your wounds I will heal, says the LORD" (Jeremiah 30:17 ESV).

We are giving the needy and hopeless hope because they don't have the necessities of survival. We have compassion, and that is why we care for the needy. Many people in Africa are struggling and suffering from famines and civil strife, and others are suffering from physical abuse or sexual abuse. Everywhere in Africa, people are crying for help. That's why we hear the cry of the hopeless and the needy. Millions are suffering from stress or depression because of the many problems in their lives. I have personally met desperate people who have reached the point of committing suicide to escape their problems.

Many go to bed hungry and wake up without being sure of their next meal. Others have much anxiety about their lives, because they have many family problems and emotional struggles in their lives. Many fear to face another agonizing day, and they have come to a place where they feel there is no way out. That's why we have many people committing suicide in the slums and the ghettos. They find the world to be against them or crumbling around them. So they are unable to bear it anymore. They are physically and emotionally exhausted. All those people who commit suicide do so because they are depressed.

Reality becomes distorted, so they see only the negative side of their problems.

Depression is caused by calamity after calamity. The victims are unable to cope with their terrible problems and evil situations. Others are depressed by being overwhelmed by the powers of the devil through witchcraft. The spirit of witchcraft affects their minds, spirit, and emotions. Many victims cry alone in their darkness, not knowing the way of deliverance. Many people are living with an inner cry in the soul that can lead them to heartbreak or heart attack.

Another thing that is disturbing people's lives in Africa is the pressure within marriage. We are living in an age when the breakdown of marriages has become increasingly prevalent, and many families are now acknowledging the dreadful social consequences of this trend. It is very sad to note that many marriage vows are no longer taken seriously by people. Relationships are becoming cold, and considerable misery is only the result. Many people today are running their homes without any regard for God. We are witnessing the collapse of family values. This is seen even in the church of Christ.

We are living under pressure in the evil world of today. We have many needs that must be met and targets to be reached. We have ladders to climb at home. We have so many things that need our attention in the family.

Another ever present problem in the home is the financial pressure. Married couples have bills to be paid. We must be good managers of our financial affairs. We must not live extravagantly until we run into debt. Remember that financial pressures are the source of disagreements in the family, and this can cause stress in marriages.

Another thing is the pressure of having many children. Many families in Africa are suffering from the stresses of having many children. You will note that your home will not be the same after the first child arrives. Pressures caused by having many children make the husband feel neglected by the wife, because she gives so much attention to the children that she has no time for her husband. The wife becomes harassed with the demands of all those little children. She is always working at home to meet the high demand of the family without a break. So these pressures can cause misunderstandings at home.

Through the preaching of the gospel, I am able to reach many souls. I am willing to restore many marriages. I use many ways to show love to the needy. A smile and a helping hand are appreciated by the needy. In Christ, we have hope.

After receiving Jesus Christ in their souls, many people go home with the full assurance that God will meet their needs. They believe that God is alive. Out of this evil world, new hope is born in the lives of people—no one is hopeless who puts their hope in God. With Christ as the center of your life, He will keep your hope flowing. This is the secret of coping with all those pressures in this hurting world.

I have seen many people come to Christ by preaching the gospel to them and giving them my personal testimony. I have sacrificially invested my life to serving the needy in love.

Serving the needy and preaching the gospel is adventurous to the end. But I am always ready to face every adventure with Christ. I will never fear because God has promised to be with me. I can fight all the visible and invisible armies of the evil one. The Bible encourages me, "Do not fear...those who are with them" (2 Kings 6:16 NKJV).

God has given me the power to preach the gospel, which makes me bold in fighting the devil. I am ready to preach in and out of season. I depend on the leading of the Holy Spirit in the ministry. I am expecting more revelations concerning the ministry from God. Jesus Christ has given me the power to do His works. "Verily, verily, I say to you,

He that believes on me, the works that I do shall he do also; and greater works than these shall he do" (John 14:12 KJV).

God's power to do His works is working in my life. I believe the Word, and Jesus released His power in my life. God didn't give me the spirit of fear, but of power, love, and a sound mind (2 Timothy 1:7).

This power has made me strong, and I can resist the devil regardless of the circumstances in life. I cannot rely only on my head knowledge or my abilities to achieve success in winning souls. I totally depend on the leading of the Holy Spirit. I was delivered from fear and intimidation. I can now pray for the sick and cast out demons in Jesus' name. The word of God encourages me, "Behold, I give unto you power to tread on serpents and scorpions, and over all the power of the enemy; and nothing shall by any means hurt you" (Luke 10:19).

God has used me in the ministry, and He has given me new strategies to battle with life. My mission: I preach Christ. The power of the Holy Spirit can take me from my current level of experience to a higher level. I was always original. I could not copy any servant of the Lord. I know that I'm unique to God, and He is ready to use me for His glory. I am His treasured vessel of honor.

I trust Him completely to fit me in His wonderful ministry. God has chosen me to preach Christ, and His power is flowing in my life. I will keep on drinking in His never failing springs. As I learned to trust in God, my ministry increased. I can't be ashamed to preach Christ. He guides, directs, empowers, and endows me with spiritual gifts. I have been experiencing different kinds of manifestations in the ministry. I will never be bound by the traditions of men in their denominations. I will move on with Christ in the ministry.

I preach hope, and I prepare people to meet Christ in the air when He returns. That's why I am echoing the cry— "Africa belongs to Christ! Africa, wake up, arise and shine, for your light has come."— I am a messenger of hope.

CHAPTER FOUR

I PREACH HOPE

My mission to the needy began with a handful of believers, and today we have grown into a big project. We can resist opposition coming both from within and from outside the ministry. I have divine approval that God has called me in this life saving mission in Africa. Africa is waiting for the most incredible outpouring of the Holy Spirit in the body of Christ.

Peace is rare in our continent today. We are hearing terrible stories of civil wars, famines, floods, disasters, calamities, tragedies, sexual abuses, child abuses, and the HIV/AIDS pandemic.

Many people are living in a harsh and challenging situation. Some have lost hope, and others are unable to bear the suffering or the pain anymore. Many people are wallowing in despair, because every day they are experiencing increased suffering in their lives. Every day the devil is leading people into more trouble. But no matter the complexity of the issues people are battling with, we are ministering hope and new life to them.

The devil plans to engage people into the battle and push them until they are at the point of being at their wit's end. The devil desires to kill and destroy many lives, but Jesus comes that we might have life, and have it more abundantly. We have hope in Africa, for we have power over all the forces of the enemy. We are giving people hope. To those who are pushed to the extreme we say, "Be strong, and do not fear, for your God is coming to destroy your enemies. He is coming to save you" (Isaiah 35:4 NLT).

The devil is causing tragedies, crises, and all the troubles that are beyond our control. The devil is making many people's lives unbearable. Evil people are causing suffering to others. Reckless people in our societies cause tribal clash conflicts and civil wars because of the lust for power. Many people are living very frustrated lives with bitterness because of evil things that were done to them. Many people are crying, and others are suffering, asking, "How long must I struggle with anguish in my soul, sorrow in my every day? How long will my enemy have the upper hand?" (Psalm 13:2). My question is— "How long will millions of innocent lives be victimized by this fatal disease, HIV/AIDS in Africa?"

How long will sorrow and pain rule our hearts because of civil wars and famine? How long will innocent people be casualties of crazy gangs of terrorists? How long must sin rule millions of people in Africa? We are battling with our sins, sorrows, and pains. We are crying for help, but we don't know the way of peace.

Amid great destruction and afflictions in Africa, I am sowing hope in the hearts of men. When Adam sinned, he was cursed, and the curse is passed from generation to generation. All our anguish, suffering, pain, and turmoil can be traced back when Adam sinned. Today we are living in a world of evil people. How are we going to cope with this evil thing around us? We are living among demon possessed people who want to drag us to degradation and have domination over us. Sin is the cause of all of our troubles and suffering in this world.

One day, I remember I was ministering in a village church, which is in one of the most crime ridden places in this area. Young people involved themselves in livestock theft. There was no running water in the area, and residents walked many kilometers to search for water. The roads were impossible during the rainy season, so you could take hours to ride an old matatus for a distance of about fifty kilometers. There were no telephone services or electricity.

I had a small church where I conducted services every Sunday and did open-air meetings in different locations in the area. Many people were saved, and the church increased daily.

In the year 1997, tribal clashes started in the neighboring community. Another tribe came to steal livestock, and the villagers resisted. They had to fight face-to-face. Life was disrupted as the raiders burned houses. The village was full of armed men fighting over livestock.

Every night women and children were screaming as the tension filled the area. Women and children fled to find refuge in the schools. In the churches, Christians were praying. God intervened, and there were fewer reports of death than would have been expected, although there were injuries and the destruction of property. In a short time, the clashes ended as the government came in to maintain security. Everywhere in the village it was calm again.

Clashes are caused by greedy people with impure motives. They are caused by corrupt people who would kill to achieve their goals. I thanked God, Who called us to give hope to those who are wounded emotionally and spiritually. "For godly sorrow produces repentance...but the sorrow of the world produces death" (2 Corinthians 7:10 NKJV). We minister to those with feelings of worthlessness and emotional scars.

Through God's unconditional love, we heal their broken hearts. We accept them as their conviction leads them to the repentance of their sins.

I used to work for God in this village church and refused to allow the villagers to seek revenge on those who had wronged them. I worked in a village where forces of darkness had a stronghold.

The government security team helped the victims return to their farms. The team asked the villagers to be calm and not to seek revenge.

Standing among all these displaced villagers, I gave them hope for survival. I told them that with God, all things are possible. No matter how bleak the situation seemed, there was still hope even though their hope seemed to be gone.

I kept on encouraging them to use the word of God. I told them that the devil had declared war in our village, but Jesus gave us peace in our troubled souls.

The villagers returned to their farms with their pangas, arrows, spears, and other weapons made from metal. You could see every person carrying his/her belongings back to their farms.

When the district officer from Gilgil came, he called all of the local communities together for a meeting. All communities lived together in peace again. Praise God.

God restored the parents who lost their loved ones. Indeed the turmoil and anguish in our village were planned to wear us down, but the Lord cared for us. He increased our strength and renewed our hope. The whole village was back to normal. God gave us peace in those evil times of unrest in our village. Our hearts sought God, and He intervened.

The Bible says we shall hear of war rumors of wars, but we should not be troubled because our redeemer lives. "For in the time of trouble He shall hide me" (Psalm 27:5).

God called me as a messenger of hope to preach hope to the hopeless. We thanked God in the village, because after prayer, there was no more bloodshed and destroying of property. Our souls are very precious in the sight of God.

After this tribal clash, I led a group of believers of all faiths in a big crusade of thanksgiving in the village. The message was entitled, "JESUS IS OUR HOPE, OUR GOD OF HOPE."

I read the message from Romans 15:13: "May the God of hope fill you with all joy and peace in believing, that you may abound in hope by the power of the Holy Spirit."

I reminded the believer that we are living amid ungodliness, violence, evil, corruption, confusion, deceit, turmoil, pain, suffering, etc. That's why we need to call upon the Lord always to sustain us.

Though terrible conditions could be around us, let's put our hope in God. The devil plans to sweep away the upright in this world through the shedding of blood. The day of our visitation is now. I will tell my enemies that I will hope in the Lord. "Do not gloat over me, my enemies! For though I fall, I will rise again. Though I sit in darkness, the LORD will be my light" (Micah 7:8 NLT).

I preached hope in the villages when other preachers preached destruction. We have new life in Jesus. We have a beautiful and everlasting home that Is made for us by Jesus Christ in heaven. We shall live there forever. You are invited,

"Come to me all who labor and are heavy laden, and I will give you rest" (Matthew 11:28 ESV).

Jesus is ready to save you from your present condition. He can restore your state and return you to your home refreshed. Are you feeling lonely and rejected? Many of our people are experiencing such feelings because of their past problems, but Jesus is ready to restore and refresh you personally.

God has good plans for you. It is the devil who is the cause of your troubles. God is able to save, protect, and guide you in your life. The Bible says, "For I know the plans I have for you...plans for welfare and not for evil, to give you a future and hope" (Jeremiah 29:11).

Jesus is our shepherd. The devil plans to steal, kill, and destroy (John 10:10). Today in Africa, the devil is stealing, killing, and destroying many innocent lives through the HIV/ AIDS pandemic.

The devil is the cause of fear, wars, conflicts, and terrorism. Many people do not sleep; they are working day and night to find new ways of killing and destroying lives. Their hearts are after the blood of men.

Through the years, I have heard of attempts to destroy the nation of Israel. Remember that the Nazis, led by Hitler in Europe, killed six million of innocent Jews. Even today, we have many groups of people who are seeking to destroy other nations.

In the Bible, we read the story of Esther, the young Jewess who stopped an attempt to destroy the Jews. Even today, I believe that Jews are a chosen nation of God, even though they are hated and rejected by many countries in the world.

In the Bible, Esther said, "For how can I bear to see the calamity that is coming to my people? Or can I bear to see the destruction of my kindred?" (Esther 8:6).

That's why I boldly declare that I do not want to see the destruction of our people in Kenya or anywhere in Africa. I must make my plea on behalf of our people. I must stand in the gap.

The people of Kenya experienced mass destruction of tall buildings, property worth millions, and people lives, as a result of a terrorist bomb blast in 1998. The media carried horrifying stories and frightening pictures on television screens. The newspapers published gruesome pictures of the scene.

You could see fire, smoke, and dust in the air. A tall building crushed the people who were caught unawares in the streets. You could see victims weeping and agonizing in great pain.

Pieces of broken concrete covered some people while the rescue workers dug frantically to recover the bodies. The emergency workers and doctors were unable to handle the great number of casualties. Many people in the city were disturbed when they saw people crying for help in great pain. The city was covered by a weighty blanket of sorrow and death.

Everywhere in the city, many people were running for safety. It was as if hell had opened its mouth to swallow many lives. You could sense the smell of terror and death in Nairobi.

The city dwellers felt as if God had forsaken them. The city was a total mess, and many people were distraught. People watched others dying without hope. Others were crying because of the death of their loved ones. What an embarrassment. It was a very terrible time in the city of Nairobi.

Many people were overwhelmed by sorrow. This was hell on earth. People in other parts of the country saw pictures on television and in the newspapers. When many saw the photos, they were angered by the evil works of terrorism. In rural areas, I saw many people who switched off their televisions to protect their emotions. They did not want to see such terrible pictures.

Do you know that today the power of evil has so dominated our present world that you can hardly hear good news from anywhere in this world? We are wondering whether this crooked generation will last. Naturally, people are asking, "Is there hope for us?"

In many nations, we hear stories of wars, suffering, disasters, tragedies, calamities, earthquakes, and famines. Many people are living in fear the world over. Evil things are unfolding before our eyes.

People are asking, "How long will innocent people suffer for nothing?" The devil is the cause of evil and suffering. The devil is causing many people to kill or destroy innocent lives. They are breaking people's bodies like toys. The blood of many people who died without cause is crying for justice.

Let us not treat sin very lightly. It is causing many people to die and others to live with permanent damages. Jesus is coming soon, and He is going to judge all sinners or evildoers.

What are you doing because you know that Jesus is coming soon? Do something to save your soul, and don't treat sin very lightly, because it is causing people to die prematurely. Sin is causing untold deaths, trouble, and much suffering in this evil filled world. Sin is a curse passing from one generation to another. There is nothing new under the sun. Because of the curse of sin, Cain killed his brother, Abel. The son of Cain, named Lamech, killed a young man, just as his father did. The Bible says, "For I have slain a man to my wounding, and a young man to my hurt. If Cain shall be avenged seven fold, truly Lamech, seventy and seven fold" (Genesis 4:23–24 KJV).

Cain was to be avenged seven times and Lamech seven times seventy. The wages of sin is death (Romans 6:23), but the gift of God is eternal life through Jesus Christ, our Lord. We hear somber stories of wars, bomb blasts, and nuclear weapons. The world is crying for justice, and God's judgment is almost at the door. He is coming to judge the evildoers and sinners. All sinners and all evildoers will be thrown into the fiery lake, which is burning with sulfur forever and ever. This place is called hell.

As a messenger of hope, I give hope to all those who are traumatized by civil wars and tribal clashes. I encourage them by telling them that God is going to judge all the wrongdoers. The misery that victims are experiencing is very different from that which the Lord will inflict openly to all the evildoers. The wrath of God will be exposed to all the haters of God.

Now is your time to receive God's mercy and forgiveness before it is too late. God's love has been passed from generation to generation. Now, let every sinner, every abuser, and every victimizer be warned that the righteous judge is standing at the door (James 5:9). What will you say at the judgment seat before the throne? Who will rescue you from the coming wrath? (1 Thessalonians 1:10).

God is always willing to pardon any repentant sinner. Christ gives every remorseful sinner immunity from eternal punishment in hell. There is hope even for all those sinners who regret the evil they have done. You can always receive forgiveness from our Father God, no matter what evil you have done.

As Christians, we have found forgiveness before our loving Father God. We know the terrible consequence of our willful disobedience. Because of our disobedience, we have a guilty conscience that makes us feel miserable until we ask God to forgive and forget our past sins. It's God who forgives the murderer and evildoer. All sins are equal before God. The wages of sin is death. Without God's forgiveness, I could have ended up in hell. I was living in despair and great disappointment, but I found rest, peace, and life in Jesus Christ by confessing and forsaking my sins. I was face-to-face with the Living Father.

I repented, which means I changed my mind as I accepted Jesus Christ as my personal savior. My soul was instantly saved, and I was overcome by God's overwhelming love. All burdens were removed from my life, and I was set free.

God forgave all of my sins in full, my case was settled, and all my sin files closed. My guilt was no more. There was no condemnation, because I was now in Christ. I was a new creature.

I was a messenger of the Gospel, and I was preaching hope to the hopeless in this hurting world. I was winning many souls for Christ in my village. I did not condemn people but rather preached love and hope. My message was about encouragement. The title was exciting: "Do not fear, only believe all things are possible to him that believes."

Jesus loves you. I will not fear. "I shall not die but live and declare the works of the Lord" (Psalm 118:17). I'm called to minister to the needy in this hurting world, and I have a lifesaving ministry. I preach hope.

CHAPTER FIVE

REACHING HOPELESS SOULS

I have learned to take all things into prayer, and even in the darkest days of my life, I will praise the Lord for Who He is, for He encourages me when I am downcast. This lesson taught me the importance of serving the needy in love. I have preached the gospel of love since God meets me at the point of my need. "The LORD is good to those who depend on him, to those who search for him" (Lamentations 3:25 NLT).

I like ministering to the elderly, the hungry, the sick, and the hopeless. I help people find peace and rest that can only be found through Jesus Christ. With Jesus Christ as my savior, what else could I need in this world? I have said that I will never wear a mask and pretend that everything is okay when people around me are dying of HIV/AIDS. I will call a spade a spade. I must do something to make a difference in this hurting world. God encourages me in the ministry when He says, "I will never leave you nor forsake you" (Hebrews 13:5 NKJV). This enables me to press on no matter the cost.

God's love awakens me to minister to others, and He gives me the oil of joy in my heart. This causes me to know Him more intimately. I have learned many ways of serving others as I see great things happen in the ministry. As I wait upon the Lord, I experience better ways of doing something more accurately, according to God's will and plan.

I want to be a man after God's own heart. I want to be a role model so that people in my ministry may change many lives, and it brings much fruit into the kingdom of God.

God called me as one of His messengers. Jesus is my love model. He shows me how to love and have mercy and compassion towards the needy and the hopeless. He rebuked the scribes and the Pharisees for being hypocrites. They neglected the weightier matters of the law: justice, mercy, and faith in the Bible (Matthew 23:23). Those three elements must be done in our ministries today.

The word of God emphasizes justice, mercy, and faith to be shown in the society to the needy, the poor, the oppressed, the disabled, the sick, widows, orphans, and the less fortunate. The Bible teaches us to follow the example of the Good Samaritan, who showed mercy, justice, and faith. He carried the injured man on the roadside, and he ministered to him. He washed his wounds with oil and paid the bill for him. He cared for him, not minding his condition or his tribe. In his heart, he helped the needy man until the end (Read Luke 10:30–37).

Jesus wants us to have mercy and not just empty sacrifices in the church. I don't want to be like the scribes and Pharisees. "For I desire mercy and not sacrifice" (Matthew 9:13).

The Bible tells me, "Learn to do good; Seek justice, Rebuke the oppressed; Defend the fatherless, Plead for the widow" (Isaiah 1:17). "Deliver the poor and needy; free them from the hand of the wicked" (Psalm 82:4).

The Bible says, "Religion that God our Father accepts as pure and faultless is this: to look after orphans and widows in their distress and to keep oneself from being polluted by the world" (James 1:27 NIV).

We are not to minister to the needy only in our area but in the whole world. All people belong to God. God upholds the widow and the fatherless (Psalm 146:9 ESV). "Defend the poor and fatherless, do justice to the afflicted and needy" (Psalm 82:3 KJV).

If God would deal with us according to who we are or where we come from, we could not survive; but we are alive because of His extraordinary grace in our lives. His mercy endures forever. "It is of the LORD'S mercies that we are not consumed, because His compassion fails not. They are new every morning: great is thy faithfulness. The LORD is my portion, says my soul; therefore, will I hope in him" (Lamentations 3:22–24). God is good, and His love endures forever. "The LORD is compassionate and gracious, slow to anger, abounding in love" (Psalm 103:8 NIV).

We are called to show mercy and compassion to the needy, just like the Good Samaritan, who helped the injured man who was suffering on the roadside. He needed help. "The LORD has told you what is good, and this is what he requires of you: to do what is right, to love mercy, and to walk humbly with your God" (Micah 6:8 NLT).

Our God is very rich in mercy, love, kindness, and justice. "Blessed are the merciful: for they shall obtain mercy" (Matthew 5:7 KJV). We should do good to all people and especially the needy. The Bible says, "For I desired mercy, and not sacrifice; and the knowledge of God more than burnt offering" (Hosea 6:6 KJV).

As we do what the Bible tells us to do, our God will do His part in blessing us, as He has promised in His word. We are His ambassadors or His messengers in this hurting world.

I am encouraged by the story of Mary, who broke her alabaster jar, which contained costly perfume. Its value could be equivalent to one year's wages those days. But she confidently broke the jar and poured the perfume on the head of Jesus, and the house was filled with the fragrance (Mark 14:3,9).

My life must be broken like that jar so that the fragrance in my soul can fill the whole world. This is an example of sacrificial love. Jesus was broken on the cross for all in this world.

I know that is not easy to be broken. The Lord uses broken people for His glory. The Bible says, "Unless a grain of wheat falls to the ground and dies, it remains alone; but if it dies, it bears much fruit" (John 12:24 NASB).

Our lives are like that grain of seed, which must die and be broken to produce much fruit. I am willing to die and be broken that I may bear much fruit and that the fruit remains. I must decrease so that Christ can increase in my life (John 3:30).

I minister to the needy and pray for them because of their problems. I prepare them to receive salvation, healing, and deliverance. Their needs become my needs, and their problems become my problems. I spend much of my time preaching the gospel to the needy and explaining to them the love of God. Needy people have physical and spiritual issues. I minister to the older people at the church and read the Bible to them.

I know many pastors who neglect the needs of the old, and I have prepared a message of hope for the old only. It is one of my responsibilities to see that the old are cared for properly. I don't just sit and feel sorry for them, but I find ways in the ministry to solve the problems in their lives. I have put the old on my shoulders, and they call me "Baba Mungu" in Kiswahili: "We love you."

Show them practical love by caring for them. If you show them God's practical love, they may be delighted to say, "I will come to your church on Sunday." Greater love has no man this that a man lay down his life for his friends. Jesus laid His life for us, so we must lay our lives for others.

We are called to win the world by showing them Christ on the cross. Christ, who is alive and who dwells in our lives. But sometimes we compromise by wearing a mask, like the scribes and the Pharisees. We have the "holier-than-thou" attitude. We are called to draw sinners to Christ. We are called to love the unlovable.

Jesus brought changes in the lives of the sinners and the needy. This ministry is very different from that of the scribes and the Pharisees. They were very selfish, and they had their self-righteousness. But they had none of God's love in their hearts. God's love never fails, for it cost Jesus His own life. We are called to love others as we count the cost.

The world needs the living God. There is great joy in heaven when one sinner repents. We are called to bring in God's fold, the lost sheep. Jesus is the Great Shepherd. We are to feed the hungry. The biblical example of our ministry can be found in: "Then the righteous will answer him, 'Lord, when did we see You hungry and feed you, or thirsty and give You something to drink?'" (Matthew 25:37).

The apostles decided to choose godly men full of the Holy Spirit, faith, and a good report. They distributed food and other physical needs in the church. They also preached the gospel with great power. God speaks through His chosen people to meet the needs of the needy. The Spirit helps them in ways to meet their needs.

When I obeyed the voice of God to go to the city, the Holy Spirit helped me to launch a humanitarian project for the needy. Since then, I depend on God for guidance. I have discovered that the needs of the rural folk are very different from that of the city folk. When I recognized real needs, I was very effective in my ministry to the needy.

The early church was very active in the ministry of love. They were concerned about winning souls, and they were very effective in meeting the physical necessities of the needy. The deacons cared for the physical requirements of the needy around them.

They were not focused on building big churches but on meeting human needs. My desire is to meet people's needs. My ministry is to make the brokenhearted rejoice in the Lord.

"The joy of the lord is your strength" (Nehemiah 8:10 NKJV).

The kingdom of God is joy, peace, and righteousness, which is brought by the Holy Spirit (Romans 14:17).

I have a burden for the needy in my heart. I don't pretend to be good, but God's love makes me sacrifice myself to serve others. I have given up everything, instead of keeping all things for myself. God's love is great in my life. I use most of my time in winning souls for Christ. I am a soldier of hope to the hopeless. Our uniform shows that I am a soldier In the kingdom of God. With love, I give the mandate of hope to the needy. I enlisted in God's army. I know that I must take some risks, and the great risk is loving the unlovable. Ultimately, His love drives me into the field to serve the needy.

Though the ministry of love, the needy can know that we are God's chosen people. "By this, all will know that you are My disciples, if you have love for one another" (John 13:35).

I minister to the needs of others without monetary consideration. My primary motive is love without compensation. I have seen pastors volunteering to serve the needy with wrong motives, but soon they become bankrupt. Ministers who work for God for wages will always complain. But if you work for the grace of God, you will find joy and satisfaction in your heart. The Bible says, "The just shall live by faith" (Romans 1:17).

Just imagine the Creator of all things using us as His chosen vessel of blessings to others, and especially the needy. I am glad to know that the almighty God uses me for His divine purposes in this world. I have given my body as a living sacrifice. I have given God my all, my life, and all of my fortunes. I have made a permanent decision to serve Him in my life. I am determined. "For where your treasure is, there your heart will be also" (Matthew 6:21).

There is no greater joy than that of serving the needy and giving hope to the hopeless. The joy of the Lord is always upon me. We do encourage those who are in turmoil.

I find greater fulfillment by building and strengthening relationships with the needy and making joy flow in their hearts.

Sometimes I contemplate— what a great love! Jesus demonstrated His greatest love to us. What shall separate me from Christ? I am more than a conqueror through Him Who loved me. I will glorify His name in my life.

I encourage the needy to fix their eyes on Jesus Christ. Focusing on their problems will increase their suffering, but with the power of God, we turn problems into opportunities. Love is not in words but in actions. When I married, I started saying to my wife, "I love you!" But these words could be meaningless to her without me demonstrating my love for her. Our relationship grows stronger every day.

I want to say that to love is to serve the needy, and I must turn my love into actions. God opens my eyes to see the needs of others around me. Genuine compassion means love in action. The needy must see your actions to understand God's love. We have all heard the story of a very famous woman called Mother Teresa. She was always busy ministering in the overcrowded city of Calcutta, India. Her ministry of love touched many great leaders. We need to serve the needy like this famous woman.

I can find my own Calcutta in my local area. I serve the needy in whatever location I am needed. Remember that the needy are always within your area. Many needy people are looking for salvation, healing, and deliverance.

Go out into the area around you and tell them the great things that God is doing for you by faith. By helping the needy, you could be making the world a better place for others to live. According to the scriptures, the world begins in our neighborhoods, and every person is our neighbor. I know there many people out there who are waiting for your encouragement. Sometimes suffering people need cheerful faces of appreciation to lift their emotions. Kind words could be like good music in the ears of a person with a heavy heart. You are a channel of blessings. Share the good things God has shown you with the person next door.

Let the needy know the love of God. When you willingly give to the needy, you get blessings in return. You will only reap what you have sown. "Let us not grow weary in doing good, for in due season we shall reap if we do not lose heart (Galatians 6:9).

God has given me a ministry of love that will never fail. I have great peace in my soul, although some people do not understand me.

I have a resource that can never be out of stock. Sacrifices are the true measure of my giving. I don't complain, even when I am struggling to raise money for my ministry's need amid hardships. But I rejoice after seeing the starving people coming to Jesus Christ. I have denied my family their comfort to get money to serve the needs of the others. I am similar to Moses, who was a good example of self-denial.

I have chosen to identify with God, rather than enjoy the pleasures of the world for a season. With God's love, I don't ask how much I will gain, but now much I will give. I always count the cost. I am concerned with other people's needs. I find things to benefit other people. My involvement in the needs of others makes me go to some dangerous places.

I am helping millions of people who are searching for inner peace. I help even those who are desperate. A life lived for God leaves a lasting legacy.

My life takes on a new meaning when I give myself to serving others. I'm generous with my time and with my resources. Because I have consecrated my life to God, I am moving forward at the impulse of His love. This highest kind of giving comes from the depth of my soul.

We are caring for people with disabilities, and we are giving to distribute food in our rescue mission; no service to the needy is insignificant. God is Love. We are serving others in His love and for His glory. I have committed my ways to the Lord, and I trust that my dream will come to pass.

I know Jesus was here on earth, and He chose to identify with the poor and the needy. He lived without a home to call His own (Matthew 8:20). But His mission in this hurting world was marked by compassion to the needy.

I have said yes to this ministry to the needy. The Bible says that when you welcome strangers in your home, you may be welcoming angels without knowing. Giving or sharing resources with others is a critical ministry before our Lord Jesus Christ, Who loves all people. Answering their cry is a mission from God. Our ministry to the needy should be marked with qualities of gentleness, compassion, love, tenderheartedness, and generosity. We do let the needy see Jesus in our lives. We serve a living God, and the Holy Spirit dwells in our hearts.

Jesus said, "I tell you, use worldly wealth to gain friends for yourselves, so that when it is gone, you will be welcomed into eternal dwellings" (Luke 16:9 NIV).

We are using all the available means to preach the gospel and reach the needy in love. We are hoping to reap eternal dividends. One day the needy will greet me with great joy at heaven's door. I want to be a good and faithful steward of what God has given me, called to be generous in meeting other people's needs. Worldly riches have eternal value only when we use them to bless others. Christ has made a tremendous impact on the needy. A little kindness by Christians speaks very loudly to the needy, much louder than a fiery sermon. A Christian's kind action is a living sermon.

People are suffering from famine, tribal clashes, civil wars, conflicts, and economic uncertainty. The devil is roaring in Africa, looking for somebody to devour. Our mission begins at home by giving hope to the hopeless, saving many people from sin, oppression, suffering, pain, tears, turmoil, famine, wars, anguish, and financial problems.

CHAPTER SIX

BLESSED ARE THE PEACEMAKERS

Everywhere in the world today, people are crying for peace in their families, schools, colleges, and in the nations.

Jesus said, "Blessed are the peacemakers" (Matthew 5:9 NKJV). That's why, as a messenger of peace, I am calling spiritual leaders to preach peace in the churches and our communities. The apostle Paul speaks to the body of Christ about this vital message, "Pursue peace with all people, and holiness, without which no one will see the Lord" (Hebrews 12:14).

We are called by God to preach in the villages, towns, cities, communities, and the nations. Everybody is craving peace. I sound a wake-up call to all spiritual leaders to preach peace. Jesus is the Prince of Peace. We, the church, had to pray in Kenya for the post-election violence to stop, and the principals signed the national accord in February 2018. Prayer works.

In the elections of 2017, when the principals disagreed concerning the elections, the spiritual leaders called for nationwide prayers, and the principals met and made a handshake. The whole country rejoiced in February 2018.

It is the primary responsibility of spiritual leaders to pray for every government to provide its citizens with security for their lives and properties. Kenya is geared towards achieving its vision in 2030.

Our ministry is joining the government and other peace organizations in training, equipping, and motivating teams of peacemakers to preach peace in our country. As church leaders, we are praying for the government to implement the new constitution. People are expecting governors and other leaders to give them effective services.

Everyone, and every community, should be ready to end conflicts or competition for power. We must all live in peace as brothers. Peace should prevail amongst us all. Let peace prevail in the whole world. Do you remember the September 11, 2001, attack on the Twin Towers in New York City, USA? What is your perception concerning world peace?

Do you pray for the countries of Kenya, Uganda, Ethiopia, Tanzania, Burundi, Somalia, Sudan, and Rwanda? Remember, the Bible says, "For when they say, 'Peace and safety!', then sudden destruction comes upon them" (1 Thessalonians 5:3).

Suddenly, the enemies of Kenya and Tanzania bombed the American embassies in Nairobi and Dar es salaam, in 1998. In the year 2002, they attacked Mombasa. In July 2015, they bombed Garissa University.

We are called as spiritual people to conduct spiritual warfare for our churches, communities, and nations. The spiritual condition of countries will determine the kind of spiritual warfare we shall do and our desire to preach peace in season and out of season. If we don't preach peace and pursue peace, we shall not see God. We should be praying without ceasing for our nations and the body of Christ. Millions are crying for inner peace in their lives. Pray until something happens.

I am leading peace forums to teach others on how to preach and pursue peace. I am a peacemaker and a peace messenger. I cannot watch the world heading in the wrong direction without preaching peace. Man's rebellious acts reveal that we are living in the last days. That's why I'm emphasizing the importance of living in harmony with each other.

May God help us so that our peace messages will expose people's sins, hidden agendas, deceptions, and evil relationships. Hidden agendas will not make us live in peace. That's why we are leading sinners to the Prince of Peace, Jesus Christ, our savior. He can set you free from sins, addictions, bondage, and evil behaviors.

Spiritual leaders should be on the front line to help the government end inter communal conflicts and insecurity over resources in all parts of our country.

In the North Rift region and the upper parts of our Kenya, cattle rustling and communal clashes are prevalent. Cattle rustling and boundary disputes are the leading causes of tribal conflicts. We should pray for our country to move quickly in disarming illegal gun holders who are fueling tribal clashes.

On peace and reconciliation, our government is implementing several initiatives seeking to provide strategic leadership and coordination in Kenya's peace agenda. The government has been carrying out some reforms to tackle these challenges in the security sector aimed at introducing accountability, professionalism, and partnership with other stakeholders, including spiritual leaders.

If you are a spiritual leader like me, I know you witnessed the worst post-election violence in Kenya in the year 2007–2008. Today we have the opportunity to learn from this and strive to make successes where we had failed in the past years. I was flashing back to those dark years, and I was awed at just how violent Kenyans were.

From my observation, I can say those spiritual leaders did not pray at all. Many of them involved themselves in politics. We are called to pray in advance to stop violence before it happens. What is violence? It is the intentional use of physical force or power, threatened or actual, against oneself, another person, or against a group or community that either results or has a high likelihood of resulting in injury, death, and physical acts, including threats and intimidation. Besides death and injury, the definition also includes violent behaviors such as psychological harm, deprivation, and maldevelopment that affect the well-being of individual families and communities.

Violence can be categorized into three categories, according to who commits the violent act: self-directed violence; interpersonal violence; and violence inflicted by larger groups such as states, organized political groups, militia groups, and terrorists. These broad categories are divided further to reflect more specific types of violence.

Self-directed violence includes suicidal behavior and self-abuse behaviors like thinking, attempting, or planning to kill oneself. However, these should not be seen as different points on a single centrum—many people who entertain suicidal thoughts never act on them, including those who attempt suicide but do not carry through with it. Many people have the intention of dying.

Interpersonal violence is divided into two sub-categories: family and intimate partners. The violence between family members and intimate partners usually takes place in the home.
This group includes forms of violence such as child abuse, violence by intimate partners, and abuse of the elderly.

Community violence between individuals who are unrelated and may know each other generally take place outside the home. This includes youth violence, random acts of violence, rape or sexual assault by strangers, and violence in the institutional settings such as schools, working places, prisons, and nursing homes.

Collective violence is conducted by people who identify themselves as members of a group against another group or set of individuals to achieve political, economic, or social objectives. It takes a variety of forms, such as armed conflicts like terrorism, and other organized violent crimes.

Crimes and violence cannot be attributed to a single factor. The persistently high level of crime and violence in Kenya can only be a complex interaction of risk factors. Violence is a daily reality.

That's why I am asking people of all nations to vote wisely and keep out greedy politicians who could fuel conflicts in our beloved countries. Do you know how evil leaders can use election violence resulting in chaos, tribal clashes, and loss of thousands of lives? Any leader who would fuel general disorder in the country or any community should be voted out. Remember how children suffered, women, girls were raped or molested during the post-election violence?

In towns and cities, businesses and shops were looted and destroyed. Many tourist hotels were closed, and the country lost billions of Kenyan shillings in cancellations of bookings by tourists. Many hotel employees were laid off.

People were killed, and others displaced, camping in schools and stadiums. I witnessed several deaths, and I saw people looting shops. I could not return home to my family in the rural area until the curfew was lifted. All those who looted were arrested by police and taken to cells. Tension continued to increase in the country as armed vigilante groups mounted patrols for self-protection. Classes in schools, colleges, and businesses were suspended.

Remember that as I'm writing, there are over ten million refugees and over 2.5 million internationally displaced people. Most of the refugees are women and children. Africa has hosted the majority of the world's refugees and internally displaced people.

That's why I'm calling our holy God to intervene and bring justice to the world. He will come to judge the world in righteousness. I know one of these days, people will be trembling with fear when God comes to rule the world with His power and justice. God is commanding everybody in the world to repent, because the time for playing games in the world and religions is over.

Another insecurity factor is the abuse of drugs and the consumption of illicit brews in the country. It is destroying the lives and the future of our youths. The youth are perpetrators of crime, rape, and other evil behaviors.

During the elections, illicit brews increased as the highest form of entreating the youth to vote for leaders. Their families and the village elders lamented the increase of deaths due to the consumption of illicit brews in the communities.

That's why I am campaigning against drug abuse and the consumption of alcohol in Kenya. My campaign is dubbed, "I shall not die but live and declare the work of God" (Psalm 118:17 KJV). There is hope for your survival.

I'm telling the youth that there is death in the pot of illicit brew. In the drinking dens, you will find young wives looking for their husbands, and you can see them carrying them home like useless cargo. Many victims of drug abuse are committing suicide, and others experience a mild form of madness if they survive.

A day doesn't pass in the villages or estates without burying a drug addict or witnessing the police collecting a dead body after a suicide.

The Bible describes the condition of the victims: "'There is no peace,' says the LORD, 'for the wicked'" (Isaiah 48:22).

I am helping the victims to recover from addiction, because it is a disease. We are rehabilitating victims in our centers and praying with them for total deliverance, in the name of Jesus. God's love and peace bring complete wholeness and rest in their souls. The Bible says, "You will keep in peace those whose minds are steadfast, because they trust in you" (Isaiah 26:3 NIV).

Let's all trust in God, and our soul will have rest and peace. To me, peace is not a promise but my possession. I have the peace of God in my soul. I have peace because the Prince of Peace, Jesus Christ, lives in my soul.

I am helping many with universal obsessions, stress, strain, stressful conditions, and even suicidal thoughts. I'm leading them to Jesus Christ, the only hope of the world.

If you look at people outwardly, you will think that they are okay, but inwardly they are hurting. That's why Jesus said, "Come to Me, all you who labor and are heavy laden, and I will give you rest" (Matthew 11:28 NKJV).

Take your burdens of sins, addictions, bondage, and evil behaviors to Jesus Christ and find rest and peace. Turn to Jesus Christ before turning to psychiatrists. The root cause of human restlessness is sin. As we accept Jesus Christ as our savior, we receive the inner peace that transcends all understanding (Philippians 4:7). Jesus gives inner peace (John 14:27).

The greatest need for all people is inner peace. A psychiatrist will tell you that the anxiety in your soul is because of an indisputable reality of everyday living. The lives of many souls today are full of tensions, hypertension, frustration, and fear. Inner peace is based on a right relationship with God through His son Jesus Christ. Do you have this relationship with Him?

The world is tired of greedy leaders with their political competitions that cause chaos and violence. We are tired of leaders inciting or giving inflammatory statements. We need leaders of integrity and justice for all. We need leaders who will rule with more liberty, justice, and progress.

God has given you the power to choose the right leaders who are relying on your vote. Don't vote collectively but individually. Choosing a leader is like signing a contract with him or her to serve you well for five years. If you are not satisfied with their service, you can withdraw the contract.

Through peace forums, we are helping to eliminate many social evils in our society. I believe in the peaceful coexistence of all communities and all faiths in Kenya. I also advocate for social justice, equitable distribution of resources, poverty eradication, and HIV/AIDS prevention.

Are you suffering from deep hurts in your soul and life? In Jesus Christ, there hope for you. He is ready to turn your weeping, your pains, and your hopelessness into inexpressible joy.

Are you mourning your loved ones' death, as Mary and Martha did for Lazarus? They mourned for four days, but when Jesus Christ showed up, Lazarus was resurrected. People saw him dead, and after a few minutes, he was alive.

I am speaking to your dead situation or condition, and I'm declaring life in Jesus Christ. I rebuke every hindrances, barrier, setback, failure, disease, fear, and frustration in your life. The Bible has given us the power to use the name of Jesus Christ in declaring anything: "You will also declare a thing, And it will be established for you; So light will shine on your ways" (Job 22:28).

That's why I declare peace in your life, peace in Kenya, and peace in our neighboring countries. Blessed are the peacemakers. Make every effort to live with all people in love and holiness, without which one will not see God.

Healing hurting souls

IF YOU ARE CRYING AND weeping in your soul over deep hurts, I have a word of encouragement for you. The Bible says, "'For I will restore health to you And heal you of your wounds,' says the LORD" (Jeremiah 30:17).

In this book, you will learn how you can be totally restored and healed from your deep hurts. Jesus Christ wants to restore your health and heal your wounds, both spiritually and physically. There is hope for you.

Having lived through so many hurts, trials, tragedies, and disappointments in my life, I know how to minister healing spiritually and physically. I have been ministering healing to spiritual leaders in my ministry. I apply the holistic, bottom-up approach in healing.

I have many moving testimonies of those who have been healed by Jesus Christ in our ministry. Do not be intimidated by your deep hurts. Trust God, through Jesus Christ, to heal you.

Are you suffering? Are you in the valley of despair? Call Jesus Christ to heal you now! Jesus Christ will never let you down.

CHAPTER SEVEN

THE PEACE MESSENGER

Kenya has experienced several terrorist attacks since December 1980 at Norfolk. In the year 1998, they attacked the United States embassy building, and in the year 2002, they attacked Kikambala in Mombasa. In the year 2014, they attacked the Westgate Mall; and Garissa University, in 2015.

That's why I have decided to be a messenger of peace. I preach the gospel of peace, telling all people that Jesus Christ is the only Prince of Peace in this hurting world. In the Bible, we read, "For unto us a child is born, Unto us a Son is given; And the government will be upon His shoulders. And His name will be called Wonderful Counselor, Mighty God, Everlasting Father, Prince of Peace" (Isaiah 9:6).

The world is striving to find peace. What is peace? Peace is the absence of mental anxiety. It's the state of living in harmony and serenity. Its freedom from war and fighting.

This is why, as a pastor and bishop, I am speaking and preaching about this important topic in various peace forums in our communities around the country. I am a peace ambassador or a peace messenger.

I'm working hard every day to provide a very comprehensive mechanism for resolving any outstanding disputes through conflict resolution meetings. I am giving victims of tribal clashes hope for survival.

I was nicknamed "The Peace Messenger" for my prominent role in peace building in the communities. I had an outstanding performance in handling difficult issues related to family and community conflicts.

Cattle rustling, communal clashes, and terrorism are prevalent in our country, and that's why I am calling my fellow Kenyans to live peacefully. People in all parts of Kenya are yearning for peace. Security agencies and the peace messengers are working together to preach peace in our beloved country.

Among the various national security challenges, terrorism stands out as one of the most sophisticated and challenging issues to handle. It has multiple manifestations across all sectors of our society and in our economy. It is a human imposed disaster aimed at making random destruction to achieve a political objective.

That's why I was called and ordained by God to preach peace and reconciliation. I'm working with anybody willing to help, along with the government, in the peace agenda. I'm doing peace forums and peace campaigns in all communities.

In my simple research, I have come to discover that alcohol consumption and drug abuse continue to pose a major threat to national peace and security, negatively affecting the economic well-being of our country.

The youth, who are the most affected, pose a severe threat to the productivity of the working age-group. Juveniles tend to engage in crime as a way of raising funds to sustain their drug dependency. The youth have formed organized criminal gangs with different names operating in villages, towns, and counties.

I am calling all people anywhere in our country and in the world to live in peace. I'm helping different communities to find reconciliation through my peace forums and peace campaigns. Since the blessed day God called me into this ministry, I have been preaching peace in this hurting world. I'm very bold because I know the One who called me. "For I know that my Redeemer lives" (Job 19:25).

Hurting and hopeless people need God's word to encourage and comfort them. They need somebody who can listen to them. I know how to encourage the brokenhearted because I was brought up in a poverty-stricken family. I know what other people are experiencing in this world.

Jesus Christ is my role model in encouraging and comforting the brokenhearted. Jesus is willing to meet everybody's needs. He said it is not the healthy who needs a doctor, but the sick. He came to call sinners, not the righteous.

From 1992, I have been preaching peace and giving hope for survival to the hopeless. I have been reconciling tribes involved in tribal clashes and resolving conflicts. I have helped the displaced victims to resettle back in their farms. Skirmishes bring cattle rustling, and cause bags of maize and other types of stored food to be destroyed.

I have learned valuable lessons that have helped me to help others in seasons of adversity. Are you suffering in your life, and maybe you do not know what to do? Read this book, and your life will never be the same again.

May the word of God encourage you. "Weeping may endure for a night, But joy comes in the morning" (Psalm 30:5). God can change your weeping into joy. I am helping the messy, wimpy people to find inner peace in their lives. God has given me a vision of hope for Africa like Joseph, who had a vision for Egypt. That's why I am saying, "Africa, do not weep. Awake! Arise! And shine, for your light has come."

After wandering in the wilderness for a long time, it is time for Africa to go into God's promised blessings. With God, everything is possible. I have written this message of hope to rekindle a blazing fire of new hope for the hopeless. This message will revive the brokenhearted.

I want God to deliver many in Africa from the spirit of fear, worries, despair, and anxiety. My message of hope is meant to aggressively restore the hurting from the sufferings. Amid turmoil, disasters, calamities, and wars, we are going to survive because God is in control.

The Bible says, "Pursue peace with all people, and holiness, without which no one will see the Lord" (Hebrews 12:14).

We are teaching the youth the importance of living in peace for they are the future leaders. We are teaching them practical ways of becoming responsible, instead of throwing them to corrupt leadership like a bone that is thrown to the dogs.

Peace is paramount in leadership. Peace can be defined as a state of living in harmony between people or groups. War is an open conflict between two or more parties, nations, or states. Today there are bad leaders inciting communities to war.

The word peace to us is not a dream but a reality in our lives. I have discovered that some of the factors that contribute to tribal clashes are bad politics, a religious sphere of influence, ethnic group leaders, and competition to rule or have power.

We have been reading daily in the papers and watching on television how all these factors mentioned have brought misunderstanding among our communities. Our country has been devastated politically, socially, and economically by greedy leaders.

Why don't we learn lessons from our neighboring countries like Sudan and Somalia? I'm pushing on despite the frustrations and setbacks. I have steadily developed as a peace messenger.

I have a peacemaking ministry. God has given me wisdom, methods, and machinery for terminating conflicts which have taken many forms in our communities. The youth are helping us in our peacekeeping mission by writing and singing songs of peace during our peace forums.

We hold big open meetings for peace and pray after the sessions. We have chosen peace representatives from every area. Recently we had a peace forum in Sirikwa Hotel in Eldoret. The agenda was peace. We invited local artists to sing songs of peace as preachers preached the same message to the people in the meeting. The meeting ended with a word of prayer.

I am working together with Rev. Kimeli from Eldoret, Rev. Koech from Moisbridge, Pastor Njenga from Molo Town, Rev. Bilgen from Lodiani, Rev. Langant from Bomet, Pastor Koskei and Julie Kirui from Olenguruone, Rev. Kimoi from Kabarak, Pastor Njoroge from Ravine, Pastor Henry Mburu from Nakuru, and Ole Kanuthu from Mau Narok, to plan meetings of peace and reconciliation in the whole of Rift Valley.

Evangelist Paul Kirui, a local artist and movie producer, sponsored peace concerts and sang songs of reconciliation. The meeting had representatives from all communities. We are peacemakers in Kenya. Our mission is to reach the whole country. We are challenging the youth to be peacemakers. We advise the youth to use their talents to live in peace with their neighbors. We are preaching peace in Uganda, Kenya, Tanzania, the Democratic Republic of the Congo (DR Congo), Rwanda, and Sudan.

I tell the youth openly to follow the steps of Jesus Christ, who is the author of peace. They should avoid evil political leaders who could ruin their lives and their future.

As a full-time pastor, I have refused to be influenced by evil politicians. In every election, they take advantage of our hopelessness, our frustrations, and the unemployment crises to use the youth for malicious purposes. These politicians create more stress in the lives of the youth after the election.

In my area, I have seen the youth used to campaign for these evil-minded politicians, and then they are damned after the election. Young men, stop being used to cause chaos or used to burn other people's houses. You are important in the sight of God and to your communities. Use your God-given talent and your potential to bless others.

Do something that could help you in the future and stop depending on any politician to guide your life. Stop campaigning for things you cannot solve. If you are well educated, use your intelligence to earn a living. Be focused on your life and your work. Focus on your dream, vision, or purpose in your life. God bless you.

Alcohol addiction is one significant cause of poverty. It makes the greedy politicians make oppressive policies, which include impunity, corruption, and graft. This causes the poor more pressure and stress in their lives. Poverty causes mental and family stress— dehumanizing and demoralizing a circumstance which leads to confusion, loneliness, and mental anguish.

The oppressive policies of our politicians lead to tribal clashes, civil wars, famine, conflicts, and general disorders, which result in internally displaced persons in camps.

My appeal to you is to avoid politicians that perpetuate poverty and hopelessness in our communities. They incite the youth to chaos and violence in the country. Their great scourge of wars and tribal clashes have brought untold sufferings and sorrow into our communities.

Some of the factors causing war are bad politics, a religious sphere of influence, ethnic groups or parties, and competition to rule or have power in the government.

We have read in the newspapers, and watched on televisions, how all these factors above have brought misunderstanding among nations and how such nations have been devastated. Despite the frustrations and setbacks, our ministry has steadily developed capacity as a peacekeeping and peacemaking organization.

The methods and machinery for terminating conflicts have taken many forms. That's why I am teaching the communities and the youth some practical ways of making and keeping peace in their areas. We are focusing on the Rift Valley because it was severely affected by the tribal clashes. In my ministry, peacekeeping is a crucial topic. I advise the youth not to follow bad politicians, "for their feet run to evil, And they make haste to shed blood" (Proverbs 1:16).

Follow Jesus, the Prince of Peace, instead of being used by bad politicians to kill innocent people, burn houses, and destroy property. Refuse to be influenced by these greedy politicians who take advantage of your joblessness and hopelessness to frustrate you more in your life. The Bible promises you blessings after keeping the peace: "Blessed are the peacemakers: for they shall be called the children of God" (Matthew 5:9 KJV).

Prophecy is a ministry gift given by Christ to bring His church into maturity. Sadly, the ministry gift of prophecy is not well understood in our days. Some believe that it is nothing more than powerful preaching. It is clear from the scriptures, however, that prophets are more than good preachers. They have an extraordinary place and purpose in the body of Christ.

The ministry of the prophet started in the Old Testament. There are two main Hebrew words for prophets. "Nabii" is the basic word in the Old Testament. It means "spokesman" or "speaker." I am God's spokesman. Basically, it means that a prophet is a person who is authorized to speak for another. In the case of the Old Testament, prophets spoke for God.

"Hozeh" means "seer." It is derived from the word "to see." Prophets were also called "messengers," servants of God, and "men of God." The message of the prophet is usually called a prophecy. But it has been called a vision, burden, oracle, or "the word of the Lord."

The Greek word "prophets" is the only word for prophet in the New Testament. The word comes from the Greek words "pro," meaning "before" or "front of," and "phemi," meaning "to show or make known one's thoughts." When these words are joined together, they tell us of the operation of the gifts of a prophet today, a prophet or a messenger of God who preaches hope, love, and peace in this hurting world.

A prophet foretells, speaking forth a message from God. It is a predictive revealing of God's thoughts.

Foretelling can come in two ways: a prediction of future events that usually only God is aware of, and a revealing of the thoughts, motives, and intent of the human heart.

Some of the end-time prophesies are being fulfilled before us: wars, famines, earthquakes, natural disasters, and acute financial crises are affecting every nation on earth. Millions are dying today due to HIV/AIDS and other incurable diseases.

I want to work for God by serving others before it's too late. God has given me a vision of reaching the unreached. I will focus on my dream. Through a dream, God saved the land of Egypt from the disaster of famine.

One day I do believe that God is going to set Africa free from tribal clashes, wars, financial crises, calamities, famines, floods, and earthquakes. I know that God is going to bless Africa more than before. Africa is deprived, but I have a dream of peace for you. My dream is going to be fulfilled.

People have been mocking me, calling me the "dreamer," but I have maintained my dream, because I know it will come to pass. God has opened doors for us in Africa. We are not going to perish. That's why we are hoping and trusting God in our lives. God is bringing us out soon. We are a team of peacemakers from different churches. Africa, walk to your destination. Seek the Lord in righteousness and holiness. Repent, Africa! This is the hour of your salvation, your deliverance, your visitation, your breakthrough, and your increase. Jesus is a wonderful counselor. Jesus heals hurting souls.

CHAPTER EIGHT

FEAR NOT

Africa is reaching a political and economic crisis. Africa is experiencing diseases, earthquakes, floods, famines, civil war, conflicts, tribal clashes, natural disasters, calamities, and the spread of HIV/AIDS. The whole of Africa is in utter chaos and confusion because of these increasing crises in the nations of Africa.

I shall not fear because the Bible tells us that we are more than conquerors; we have the spirit of love, power, and a sound mind. We shall never be perplexed by what the devil is doing in the continent of Africa. In Jesus Christ, we have the answers.

The Spirit of God is encouraging us and driving us to our knees to get more strength. God is reviving us and renewing us. We have a new anointing power to drive out the devil and his battalion, reaching into the deepest hell in Jesus' name. Despite the physical effects which the devil could be manifesting in our lives, we have overcome him— that's why we are declaring full salvation and healing in Jesus' name. The Bible says, *"We will not fear...though the mountains be carried into the midst of the sea" (Psalm 46:2 NKJV)*. In every problem situation, trouble and crises end where our faith in Jesus Christ starts.

Listen to the sweetest invitation that ever fell in human ears- "Come unto me, all ye that labor and are heavy laden, and I will give you rest" (Matthew 11:28 KJV).

This is a word from God for Africa. Take all your burden to Jesus, and you will find rest. The choice is yours. You can either choose Christ or crises. This is a glorious fact. Will you believe Him right now? The Bible says of Christ- "Surely he hath borne our grief 's, and carried our sorrows" (Isaiah 53:4).

We were called to the kingdom of God when Christ won the battle for us. That is why I am aggressive to fight the devil, who is the greatest enemy in our lives. We are called to battle like King David, who, by the power of God, won the battle. "David replied to the Philistine, 'You come to me with sword, spear, and javelin, but I come to you in the name of the LORD of Heaven's Armies—the God of the armies of Israel, whom you have defied'" (1 Samuel 17:45 NLT).

Like David, we know the secrets of victory. Through the power of God, we are going to defeat the devil and his hosts. Through faith in God, we are going to defeat HIV/AIDS; this is the twenty-first century giant that is destroying millions of people. God has given us the power to defeat and resist the devil.

Once when the apostle Paul and his fellow shipmates experienced a terrible storm at sea, he encouraged them. For three days, they neither saw the sun, not stars, and the storm continued raging. They lost all hope of being saved. The storm was so fierce they could not eat. Paul encouraged them, saying, "But take courage! None of you will lose your lives, even though the ship will go down. For last night an angel of the God to whom I belong and whom I serve stood beside me, and he said, 'Don't be afraid, Paul, for you will surely stand trial before Caesar! What's more, God in his goodness has granted safety to everyone sailing with you.' So take courage! For I believe God. It will be just as he said. But we will be shipwrecked on an island" (Acts 27:22–26).

Paul had advised the people on board not to leave the island of Crete for a while, but they ignored his advice. They despised him, not knowing that he was a prophet of God. Whosoever honors the word of a prophet prospers. Paul had said, "Men, I believe there is trouble ahead if we go on—shipwreck, loss of cargo, and danger to our lives as well" (Act 27:10). But nobody took an interest in his warning. So the people on board encountered much trouble in the sea. It became stormy and windy. Lastly, Paul encouraged them that not one of them would be lost. They would be all saved.

It could be that you are experiencing a storm, maybe trials and temptations in your life. Darkness has surrounded you, and you do not know where to turn for help. Perhaps you have lost hope. Let me encourage you, don't lose hope, don't give up. Anchor your hope in Christ, and He will rebuke the storm for you, saying, "Peace be still."

Keep on believing in Him. Say like the singer, "My hope is built on nothing less than Jesus' blood and righteousness." Trust in Christ, the solid Rock of Ages. Hide your life in Him. Come and take refuge in Him.

Paul assured the people that God was going to deliver them. He told them that our God is faithful and will keep His word. Heaven and earth shall pass away, but the word of God will stand forever. The word of God, which He speaks through His servants, will not return to Him void. When the people on board saw the salvation of the Lord, the joy of the Lord filled their troubled hearts. I am called to give the hopeless hope and encouragement.

Learn to wait and trust in God at all times. Have you ever eaten ripe fruit? No doubt, you would be disappointed with the taste if you ate fruit before it had ripened. Fruit takes time to ripen, and waiting for the Lord might certainly take time, but keep on waiting for the Lord. In any circumstances, trust in the Lord.

The Bible says, "'The Lord is my portion,' says my soul, 'Therefore, I will hope in Him!' The Lord is good to those who wait for Him, to the soul that seeks Him" (Lamentations 3:24–25 NKJV).

Keep on waiting and trusting on the Lord. Blessed are those who wait upon Him. Wait for the fulfillment of His purposes in your life. Millions of people have been waiting upon Him in this hurting world.

Don't wait for Him in frustration; begin to praise Him while still waiting upon Him. The Bible says, "But I will hope continually and praise you yet more and more. My mouth will tell of your righteousness acts, of your deeds of salvation all the day, for their number is past my knowledge" (Psalm 71:14–15 ESV).

Waiting for God can be frustrating, like waiting for a delayed bus. It should be more like a young child who joyfully waits for the parents to come home with a basket full of good fruits from the market. We are to help others and encourage them to wait upon the Lord.

Waiting for the Lord involves loving and serving Him without giving up hope. This could be challenging to some of us who are called in the ministry to serve the needy and the hopeless. I would encourage all servants in the ministry to read the psalm: "I wait for the Lord, my soul waits, and in his word, I hope; my soul waits for the Lord more than watchmen for the morning (Psalms 130:5–6).

God loves all those who trust and keep on waiting on Him. "But the LORD takes pleasure in those who fear him, in those who hope in his steadfast love" (Psalm 147:11). Trust and hope in the Lord. I'm thrilled to know that Jesus is the same yesterday, today, and forever. Never before has there been such a need to encourage others and to use every opportunity to preach the good news to the lost. To continue preaching the good news in such a corrupt and hostile world requires endurance. But I would encourage you to keep on serving Him, no matter the cost.

It is time, as ministers of the gospel, to shake the devil until the people around you change their minds. Let us not compromise with the devil or nurse him. We have been given the power to cast every demon and the devil, in Jesus' name. We are called to preach the gospel so that many lost souls and the needy can receives salvation through the blood of Jesus Christ.

The time for the gospel is now. Let us stand with the promises because there is a day coming when we shall stand before the throne of God to give an account of our work in this world.

With this in mind, we must keep preaching the gospel until Jesus comes the second time. My help comes from the Lord! I will always hope and put my trust in the Lord so that on the day of the storm, I will get help from Him.

I always believe what we do for God today will determine what He will do for us in the next world. Maybe in your life now, things have rolled in a manner you cannot explain. Jesus can help you regardless of your circumstances, and you will tell others of God's faithfulness. I have seen God giving incredible financial breakthroughs to believers who have trusted in Him. They prosper after living below poverty life. Today the issue of poverty is felt by many in this hurting world.

God wants you to move the mountain before you by faith and throw them in the deepest seas. He has given you power through faith over every problem in your life. It has been a bad habit that when young people are faced with circumstances that are beyond their control, they begin to complain and cry, saying, "where is God?" instead of facing their problem by faith, taking authority in Jesus' name, and throwing that problem into the sea.

Every day on the television, radio, and in the newspaper, we receive reports of horrifying cases of drug abuse, sex abuse, murder/suicide, and tragic accidents around the world. These are some of the mountains that should be thrown into the seas in Jesus' name.

As a youth pastor, I would encourage you, the youth, to stand firm in your faith and do the works of God by faith. Everybody is waiting for you because you are strong, and the word of God is in you. I would be ready to take the weapons of God to fight and resist the devil. The devil is ruling the world. "For all that is in the world—the lust of the flesh, the lust of the eyes, and the pride of life—comes not from the Father but is from the world" (1 John 2:16).

I thank the Lord, for He has given me the power to fight and to resist the devil. By faith, I have declared war on the devil and the kingdom of darkness. I am ready to put on the whole armor of God against the tricks of the devil. I am to pull down the strongholds of the devil by using the weapons of God.

It is wrong for me to sit down doing nothing when the deadly HIV/AIDS pandemic is killing millions of our brothers and sisters. I'm going out to tell all people there is hope by calling on the King of kings, Jesus Christ, Who can stop you from sexual immorality leading to AIDS.

When the children of Israel were crossing the desert, the fiery serpents were biting and killing many of them. The Bible says that "Moses made a serpent of brass and put it upon a pole and it came to pass, that if a serpent had bitten any man, when he beheld the serpent of brass, he lived "(Numbers 21:9 KJV).

"Flee sexual immorality. Every sin that a man does is outside the body, but he who commits sexual immorality sins against his own body. Or do you not know that your body is the temple of the Holy Spirit [who is] in you, whom you have from God, and you are not your own?" (1 Corinthians 6:18–19 NKJV).

In these last days, the serpent which is called HIV/AIDS is biting many people in this world, but thank God that we have Jesus, Who is the brass serpent; when He is lifted up, whoever is bitten by the serpent (HIV/AIDS) and looks up to Jesus is saved and has eternal life. In Jesus Christ, we have hope for salvation from sin and diseases, which are caused by the old serpent, the devil, and his lot. "As Moses lifted up the serpent in the wilderness, even so must the Son of Man be lifted up, that whoever believes in Him should not perish but have eternal life" (John 3:14–15).

The word of God makes you strong to overcome the devil. Flee sexual morality. "Therefore submit to God. Resist the devil, and he will flee from you" (James 4:7).

CHAPTER NINE

JESUS OUR BLESSED HOPE

In Africa, we are living the most common emotion—fear in our lives. Every day, death is threatening our lives as diseases and evil things are happening in our beloved continent,

Fear is contributing to rapid heartbeats, nervousness, high blood pressure, and heart problems. Nowadays, the effects of anxiety are severe and devastating.

Fear is leading many of us to instability and unhappiness. Sin causes fear. When Adam sinned, he was in hiding, and God called him and asked why he was hiding. Adam said, "I was afraid" (Genesis 3:10). We are living in fear because everywhere we look, we see signs of moral decay. People are suffering in great pain because of their sins.

In the Bible, we read that when the children of Israel sinned in the days of Moses, "the LORD sent fiery serpents among the people, and they bit the people; and many of the people of Israel died. Therefore the people came to Moses, and said, 'We have sinned, for we have spoken against the LORD and against you; pray to the LORD that He take away the serpents from us.' So Moses prayed for the people" (Numbers 21:6–7).

The same thing happened in the days of the prophet Jeremiah. The Lord sent a strong message to His people saying, "For behold, I am sending among you serpents, adders which cannot be charmed, and they shall bite you" (Jeremiah 8:17 ESV).

Today in every nation of the earth, the living God has released fiery serpents that are taking millions of people through sexual immorality. When the fiery serpent bites, Satan's venom, the HIV/AIDS virus, passes into your body, and you die of AIDS.

Many people are living careless lives in sexual sin, much like the children of Israel. That's why people are suffering from signs of fiery serpents. AIDS is the judgment of God. Who can heal the judgment of God?

Moses was commanded by God to make a bronze serpent and set it on a pole. Later, the Bible says that Jesus is the bronze serpent that was lifted up in the wilderness by Moses. So when you look at it, you are saved and healed from your sins by Jesus. The Bible says, "As Moses lifted up the serpent in the wilderness, even so must the Son of Man be lifted up, that whoever believes in Him should not perish but have eternal life" (John 3:14–15).

The Bible says that you are suffering as a result of your sins. You are sick from your feet to your head. "He who digs a pit will fall in it, and a serpent will bite him who breaks through a wall" (Ecclesiastes 10:8 ESV). Stay within the walls of your holiness and righteousness. Stay within the walls of your marriage.

My long-term dream is to give the needy a new purpose and destiny. I will focus on and concentrate on my vision. I will remain original, and I will not copy anybody. I will prayerfully listen for guidance from my God, for my sole desire is to please God. I will preach the undiluted word of God, which will impart life to the needy.

It is a fact that Africa is shaped like a question mark, but Jesus is the answer for Africa. God knows about every problem and crisis in Africa, and He has a solution for every issue concerning the needy. Because Jesus is alive, we are going to survive. We are indeed troubled on every side, but we are not destroyed. It seems that Africa is at a crossroads, but God is our refuge in every storm. Our help is coming from above, from the King of kings.

Jesus can help us because He was once on the cross, surrounded by the murderers with no escape from death. Even one of His disciples denied that he knew Him. Jesus patiently endured the cross, and He conquered all things, including death. That's why we are preaching Christ, for He is the same yesterday, today, and forever.

I began my ministry at home because I believe charity begins at home. I am setting the needy free from oppression, suffering, pain, tears, turmoil, anguish, and financial burdens. We started the ministry with a handful of believers in the village, and we are growing spiritually and expanding to other towns and cities.

We can resist the powers of the devil which come against us from within and outside the ministry. We have approval from above that God has given us this wonderful life saving mission. We survive through challenging conditions, and God gives us the strength to press on.

We are able to rescue all those who are at a point of losing hope, because the devil is leading them into more trouble. But no matter the complexity of the issues, we are battling to minister life and hope. We are called to help them battle with the power of darkness as we save them even when they are at their wits' end. The devil plans to destroy their lives, but we are given authority over the powers of the devil and bind him to the extreme. We are to encourage them. "Say to those who with fearful hearts, 'Be strong, do not fear, your God is coming'" (Isaiah 35:4 NLT).

In Africa, most of the greatest tragedies and crises are caused by human beings. People are used by the devil to cause conflicts and wars, making life unbearable. Most of our problems come from human beings because of carelessness, selfishness, and lust of power. At first, a man pretends to be very sweet in his speech, but it causes troubles and conflicts to the hearers.

Many people are living with a lot of bitterness due to the evil things which were caused by others in their lives. Many people are dying without hope; others are asking the question, "How long must I take counsel In my soul and have sorrow in my heart all the day? How long shall my enemy be exalted over me?" (Psalm 13:2 ESV).

How long shall evil-minded leaders exploit innocent people? How long shall the deadly epidemic, HIV/AIDS, victimize millions of innocent lives? How long will sorrow and pain rule over lives because of civil wars and conflicts? How long shall casualties of the crazy gangs of terrorists who are wrestling with our lives make us cry for peace in Africa? We are working with organizations, and we are networking with churches and ministries.

The purpose of this network is to reach the unreached and give the needy hope in all parts of Africa. That's why we are praying and working with other leaders in the ministry, volunteers, and coordinators to accomplish this divine mission. I am willing to support and serve others in this capacity. I have created a channel in our Nairobi office for sharing resources and ideas with all stakeholders.

If you are willing to assist us in anything, do let us know, and we shall be glad to place you where you are most needed. You can kindly help us launch a very effective ministry to the needy and the less fortunate in this hurting world. We are inviting the body of Christ in Africa to come together in prayer and fellowship by forming this network. This network is very crucial because it is going to function as a central nervous system in the body of Christ in Africa. The Bible encourages me that this is possible. The Bible says, "Behold, how good and pleasant it is when brothers dwell in unity! For there, the LORD has commanded the blessing, life forevermore" (Psalm 133:1,3).

Together we are echoing the cry "Africa belongs to Christ." Let it be your cry too. More souls must be reached before it is too late. However, peace is sometimes rare in our hate filled continent. We are declaring peace in this troubled continent in Jesus's name. Let your prayer be, "Lord, turn your face toward [Africa] and give us peace." (Numbers 6:26 NIV). God's peace brings hope, and we are messengers of hope in Africa.

The word of God asks, "Who is among you that feareth the LORD, that obeyeth the voice of His servant, that walketh in darkness, and hath no light? Let him trust in the name of the LORD, and stay upon his God" (Isaiah. 50:10 KJV).

Hearing the voice of God and obeying will take you out of the darkness. Let me say that sometimes the Lord allows you to pass through a season of most profound darkness. I am writing this to encourage you. Maybe you could be suffering and wondering what is wrong with you. There is nothing wrong. God allows some situations in your life so that He can show you how He cares. If you have never passed through a series of temptations and trials, the cross of Christ could have no meaning in your life.

I am encouraging the suffering, the poor, the tortured, and the anguished souls to understand what it means to wrestle with wicked spirits in heavenly places. This message is for you, you whom trials have overwhelmed. And you in the darkness so thick that it can be felt around you. Be prepared with all the weapons of our warfare, especially the shield of faith and the sword of the Spirit, which is the word of God. To others, it may be very difficult, but you, as a child of God, will be victorious. Tell the devil, "Rejoice not against me, O mine enemy: when I fall, I shall arise; when I sit in darkness, the LORD shall be a light to me" (Micah 7:8).

After experiencing the presence of God in your life, share with others the hallelujahs of your faith. You can now shout the victory of the blood of Jesus with your lips. Your former problems of poverty, bereavement, sickness, and unjust accusations from people could be the story of your past. You used to be bound in spiritual darkness, and you searched for God forward and backward, but you did not find Him. Suddenly, He appeared and delivered you from your troubles. You can praise and worship Him in your life now.

God's grace reaches further than we can imagine. Tell Him that you will surrender all to Him, so He may fill you with His wonderful blessings. Tell him that you are bankrupt and need His great grace in your life. Let Him fill you over and over again. Assure Him that you are going to trust Him in life, forever. Tell Him that you are ready to die with Christ so that you can raise with Him from the grave. Believe that His greatest love is for you. Say to Him openly that "though he slay me, yet will I hope in him" (Job 13:15 NIV). Praise the Lord, for He is faithful. The word of God says, "The one who offers thanksgiving as his sacrifice glorifies mc; to one who orders his way rightly, I will show the salvation of God!" (Psalm 50:23 ESV). Let's worship and praise God! He is our blessed hope.

The Bible encourages me to know that there is a blessed hope set before me. It is the anchor of my faith in my life. Everyone with this blessed hope in his/her heart purifies himself/herself before Christ. Do you have this hope to cleanse you from all of the filthy ways of the world as you walk in holiness in your life?

Jesus is coming soon! Are you looking for this blessed hope in your life?

Our hope is in Jesus. "Hope deferred makes the heart sick, But when the desire comes, it is a tree of life" (Proverbs 13:12 NKJV).

Get ready; the Savior of the world is coming soon. "Let everyone that names the name of Christ depart from iniquity [unrighteousness]" (2 Timothy 2:19 KJV).

"Therefore, let us not sleep as do others; but let us watch and be sober" (1 Thessalonians 5:6).

"Therefore be you also ready; for in such an hour as you think not the Son of man comes (Matthew 24:44).

Jesus is our blessed hope!

CHAPTER TEN

GOD OF HOPE

Everyone in the village was praising, worshiping, and thanking God for saving us from post-election violence. The Bible says, "Seek the LORD, all you meek of the earth, Who have upheld His justice. Seek righteousness, seek humility. It may be that you will be hidden In the day of the Lord's anger" (Zephaniah 2:3 NKJV).

Life consists of a constant battle between God and the devil. Whom do you want to have ruling over your life? Do you want God our redeemer, or the devil, the prince of this world? The decision is yours.

Our hope is in God because we are the redeemed and can pledge our wholehearted allegiance to Him. It is, therefore, necessary to daily renounce all the works of the devil before we start the day. We must not be ignorant of his devices. Every day I must commit my life to God together with a declaration of His incredible power.

I give my entire life to Him, telling Him that I'm His. I begin the day by thanking and praising Him for His wonderful salvation through the blood of Jesus Christ. Christ lives in me!

In all things every day, I declare, "Have your way, Lord, in my life." I ask God to fill me with His Holy Spirit and help me to present my body before Him as a living sacrifice.

In the meeting in the village, we thanked, praised, and worshiped God together by faith. We shouted together, "Thank you, Lord!" After this declaration, we all yielded ourselves over to the leading of the Holy Spirit. It was precious to see peace and joy in every heart.

You could see individual families and groups of Christians praising and worshiping God together for the great things He did in our village. Praise God! Everybody left the meeting praising God for His wonderful protection. All people, both young and old, showed a heart full of thanksgiving. Villagers vowed to help one another physically and spiritually. The words from the speakers encouraged and strengthened them. Every villager felt that God is with us.

God gave us victory in evil times without using our spears, arrows, knives, or pangas. As a pastor, I thanked God personally because the power of God was evident in the village.

Months have passed since that turbulent event in the village; however, I often thank God for His extraordinary protection in our lives. The villagers learned an enduring lesson: to wait on God and trust fully in His mighty hand. Yes, like other dear ministers of the gospel in the village, I have experienced a great move of God in my life. God restored peace to our lives in the village.

After this crusade, the church experienced a powerful move of the Holy Spirit on a daily basis. The attendance of the church increased with new believers. Men, women, and children came to the church in large numbers. With great joy, they stepped before the altar to surrender their lives to Christ. Others testified of having received healing in their bodies. After prayers of faith, miracles happened in the midst of the congregation.

In the services and the weekday fellowships, God moved in many beautiful ways. You could hear Christians praising, worshiping, and having joyful celebrations together. At the top of their voices, they were shouting and declaring Jesus as the King of kings. They shouted victory, putting the devil where he belongs, under our feet.

God was doing great things in our midst, and we believed that he was going to do exceedingly more above all we were asking in our lives. The Lord was blessing us in a mighty way after that evil time when we experienced losing lives, properties, and the loss of the harvest. God brought us into a new level in our lives that we could not remember having in the past. After seeing the great things that the Lord was doing in the church, all the villagers who used to despise me now called me a prophet.

The villagers honored the word of God, and He prospered them. The village that experienced stormy times learned that we are strangers in this world and that one day we shall meet our redeemer in heaven, after leaving all possessions behind us. That's why I tell the Christians not to carry too much in this world because it might not allow them to go towards heaven smoothly. I tell them to cast all their burdens on Jesus Christ, and they will find rest for their souls. As a Christian, you should not carry any burden, because when temptations come and the storm hits you, you will not be able to move very fast.

The people of my village will never forget the storm which they experienced in their lives. The storm of clashes and darkness was all around the village. The villagers had experienced the impact of the storm. They were tossed around, and they left their homes. They went to live together in a camp ten kilometers away as refugees. Men were unable to go forward, sideways, or backward. They had lost hope to fight for their families. The servants of the

Lord prayed, and they anchored their hope in God, and salvation was experienced. The devil wanted to mess up their lives, but God intervened. I can say that there is hope for you in your evil times.

Don't be afraid when the enemy strikes in times of your storm and trouble. Those who know the Lord will not be ashamed because God knows their next move. God knows all things, and He is always ready to save His people from temptation. Many people in the village made fun of me, and they thought that I was useless. But through the power of God, they found that I am a true servant of the Most High God.

In the name of Jesus Christ, our God is able. Amid the crises, God answered my prayers, and the villagers live in peace even today. As we praise Him in the village, He dispatches His angels everywhere. The villagers know that their help comes from the Lord. The villagers used to mock the believers, but without them, they would not have made it.

It is because of the faith of the believers that they survived. God had to contact His servant Abraham before destroying the city of Sodom. The secrets of God are with those who fear Him. You don't need to care what might come your way. Simply trust and put your hope in God. All you need to know is the mind of God about you. The Bible encourages me, "Surely the Lord GOD does nothing without revealing his secret to his servants the prophets" (Amos 3:7 ESV).

I will keep on working for God, no matter the storms. I will never stop because of hindrances or obstacles. When the devil said I could not make it, I declared that I would make it, in Jesus' name. I know that the devil does not give up. He might come a second or third time or more. The good news is that I will never give up or lose hope in my life.

I know that the devil is a thief, and I will not allow him to steal anything from me. Jesus will give me more strength to resist him. I will never listen to his threats. I will spend my time praising and worshiping God for His greatness.

It's my time to shake the devil until all the people around me change their minds. I will never compromise with the devil. The time to shake the devil is now. The time for change is now. But remember it's only God through Jesus Christ Who can help you now. As a pastor and a messenger of hope, I trust that despite all the problems you could be facing, you can be sure of God's unfailing love for you.

God has been encouraging my heart from time to time. I am also very grateful when I receive encouraging letters or calls from my friends or other servants of the Lord. I'm particularly aware of the great need for encouragement to the needy, especially when they feel down or under pressure. I know many people out there who are in desperate need of encouragement.

I sometimes put the needy on my shoulders as I give them moral support. Often I go alongside them, showing them God's love in practical ways. Sometimes people turn to Christ after seeing the way we are caring for their physical and emotional needs. Meeting their needs makes them seek the Lord. We are reaching many hurting souls in this way. "Greater love hath no man than this, that a man lay down his life for his friends" (John 15:13 KJV).

The Bible encourages me, "Let us not grow weary while doing good, for in due season we shall reap if we do not lose heart" (Galatians 6:9 NKJV). With God's help, you will never lose heart and give up.

Keep on surviving in the name of Jesus, and never stop because of hindrances. When the devil announces to you that you will not have babies in your marriage, start naming babies. If the devil tells you that you are going to die, tell him, "I shall not die, but live, And declare the works of the LORD" (Psalm 118:17).

In stressful times we must put our hope in God. Let us never think of God harshly or with bitterness in our hearts because of the bad things that are happening in our lives.

Let us check our thoughts, because our evil thoughts towards God can grieve Him. Let's put aside our weaknesses and afflictions and go to Him with confidence.

Let's settle down in God's love forever. God permits all things that will bring glory to His name. This makes me sleep in peace, because I know that God has a good plan for me.

I wake up very early in the morning with good thoughts concerning God before praying. God fulfills the desires of my heart. "A desire fulfilled is sweet to the soul" (Proverbs 13:19 ESV).

When trials and temptations come my way, I seek help from God in every storm. He sees me through, for His everlasting love and care endures forever. In the midst of every turmoil, I have the keys which Jesus has given me. It is time to shake the devil. I will never compromise. I will preach hope in season and out of season.

When the whole country was experiencing election violence and tribal clashes, Jesus stood on our side. He said, "Peace be still," and everything was calm in our nation. We are surviving again. We are not wavering in our faith. We are anchored in the Rock, the unshakable Rock, the Rock of Ages, Jesus Christ!

He helps us overcome all of the storms in our lives. The word of God encourages me, saying, "Why are you cast down, O my soul? And why are you disquieted within me? Hope in God, for I shall yet praise Him For the help of His countenance" (Psalm 42:5 NKJV).

Hope in God! For with Jesus, survival is possible. Trust in the God of hope. I preach hope to the hopeless. I lead the hopeless declaring, "I shall not die, but live, and declare the works of the LORD" (Psalm 118:17).

I encourage the hopeless with God's word! Everyone who is hopeless, their hope is in God! Never lose hope!

CHAPTER ELEVEN

SURVIVAL IS POSSIBLE

We are living in the end times when people are perishing. People in some nations of the world are living in fear, turmoil, anxiety, depression, and suffering.

These are the signs of the fulfillment of the words in the Bible, which says: "There shall be signs in the sun, in the moon, and in the stars; and on the earth distress of nations, with perplexity, the sea and the waves roaring; men's hearts failing them from fear and the expectation of those things which are coming on the earth, for the powers of heaven will be shaken. Then they will see the Son of Man coming in a cloud with power and great glory" (Luke 21:25–27 NKJV).

We are living in an hour unlike any other in the history of humanity, when world leaders do not have answers for the evil things which are happening in the world today. Our cities are plagued by an epidemic of violent crimes, and gangs of armed criminals are stealing and robbing innocent people in their homes. There is also an increase of sexual insanity among women and girls, even those of a very young age.

Sexual immorality and sexual perversion are directly responsible for the spread of the HIV/AIDS epidemic that is killing millions of people in our so-called modern world.

Families are perishing for lack of food, and others are filing for divorce. People are crying for help, and some are suffering from famines, floods, wars, tribal clashes, and global conflict.

These are the signs of the end times in a demon possessed society. The dispensation is passing away, and we are in the middle of the nightmare when the world is full of evil things, and man has caused trouble in the world.

There is no peace in the air, in the sea, or on the land. Jesus is the only hope for this world. We are waiting for the dawning of the glorious day when—suddenly— Jesus, the Prince of Peace and the King of kings, shall appear in great glory in a cloud to this world. Today we are reminded that all of the problems we are facing were prophesied in the Bible. Everybody knows that Jesus Christ is coming again into this world.

The Bible says, "Jesus is the same yesterday, today, and forever" (Hebrews 13:8).

As a full-time pastor, I feel a sense of fulfillment in reaching the unreached before it is too late. My greatest desire is to reach out to the needy and the hopeless. I spend most of my time preaching the gospel and serving the needy.

One lady told me that, "No matter how much energy I put into preparing Christians to meet Christ, some still feel emptiness and disappointment during the Christmas season." Many people regret spending a lot of money on pleasures during the Christmas season. To many people, this season is somewhat meaningless, but they try to find meaning in merrymaking festivals and gift giving.

Without accepting Jesus Christ as your personal savior in your soul, Christianity will never have meaning in your life. Without Jesus Christ in your soul, you will never experience divine joy. Even though you try to participate in all the traditional activities where you are surrendered by friends and relatives, you will still be missing the joy of the Lord in your soul and will still feel an empty spot.

Let me tell you that even with all these gifts and pleasures, you will still be feeling something is missing in your life. On the surface, you could be pretending that everything is fine, but deep inside, you know that the celebrations of Christmas have no real meaning for you.

The real joy is found in the person of Jesus Christ, not the celebrations of Christmas. The joy of the Lord is not for a season, but it is everlasting. "For the kingdom of God is not eating and drinking, but righteousness and peace and joy in the Holy Spirit" (Romans 14:17).

The joy of the Lord should dwell in your soul 24/7. It should remain in you during Christmas and every day of your life. Since I accepted Jesus Christ as my personal savior, celebrations, or family get-together parties have no meaning. I'm not moved by the most prominent social events of the year in this world.

I am moved by the love of Jesus Christ, and in Him, I have experienced the joy of the Lord in my soul. Jesus is loving and everlasting. And although the celebration has a fundamental religious significance to me as a Christian, my joy comes when I am serving the needy and the hopeless during Christmas. This makes the celebrations come alive in my life.

Many people in this hurting world pretend to have joy during Christmas by indulging in various pleasures, in drinking, and in eating, but they are spiritually bankrupt. So to them, the real Christmas is devoid of meaning.

That's why I have taken my time to tell you the importance of Christmas and how the celebrations could bring you the greatest joy you could find in your life. Take your time and ask yourself, "What's most important about Christmas?" Don't rely on what people say about it or what they do during this season. Get your answer to that question directly from God.

I would advise you to make a very important choice because Christmas offers so many possibilities. Do you celebrate the birth of Christ through your sinful pleasures, in family pleasures, in joys of meeting with friends, or in creating a beautiful home environment with decorations?

All these pleasures are delightful, but cannot give you the joy of the Lord that you could find in your life. Find the real joy by helping the needy and the hopeless. Visit people in hospitals or nursing homes. Visit the orphans and homes of the elderly.

Do you have a desire to meet other people's needs and be charitable? Do works of kindness and have actions in your life that help others, because celebrations of pleasures cannot give you the real joy you need.

Choose to serve others and win souls for Christ. Without a vision in helping the needy and the hopeless, you cannot find real joy in your soul. Your joy could be fractured and superficial. You must receive Christ in your soul and focus on serving the needy and the hopeless to find joy in your life.

I have chosen to reach out to others in love during this season. Let me ask you a question. Why do you spend thousands on your pleasures in drinking and eating? This is selfishness. Christ died for the hurting and the needy souls. Why don't you celebrate His birth with the needy and the hurting? Christ died for your family, friends, and the lost.

Remember this when you are celebrating with your friends and family. People are suffering without food, and others are sick at home and in the hospital. Why should you spend a lot of money on yourself while other people are suffering around you?

Let's ask ourselves why Jesus was born, and why He died on the cross. He died to save the lost and meet the needs of the needy and the hopelessness. So reach out to others in love. Serve the needy, and don't use all your money on your own pleasure. Christ cares for others, even today. Jesus is the same yesterday, today, and forever. So when you are celebrating the birth of Christ during Christmas, remember that He changes not and that Jesus is not a young child. He is the King of kings!

Many people in this world are overwhelmed by the celebrations, and they forget to accept the King of celebrations. Accepting Jesus Christ as your personal savior in your soul could bring you the greatest joy. And to reach out to others in love could bring you the joy of the Lord.

I was called to serve others. I am energetic and very resourceful. I have chosen to reach out to others even during Christmas. My greatest desire is meeting other people's needs. I realized that a spontaneous act of generosity is more spiritually alive in my soul at Christmas when reaching out to others.

I have learned to find joy in serving the needy and the hopeless. If you find yourself not comfortable with serving others, then you can send a check to your favorite charity. This could be the best way of reaching spiritual fulfillment in your soul. I am helping you find meaningful ways to express the joy of Christmas by serving others. You can find great satisfaction in initiating acts of kindness to others. To reach out to others in love is spiritual.

Make a difference in this hurting world. Visit the sick and the needy on Christmas Eve or Christmas. Christmas is a time to show kindness to others. If you are not comfortable with being face-to-face with the sick or the needy, you can send your gifts to charity. Remember that Jesus is coming soon! He will weigh every man's virtues and sins with undivided attention. He will use a righteous scale to measure your deeds. He will dispatch the workers of evil and sinners to hell, and usher the doers of good deeds and the righteous into His kingdom, forever and ever.

That is why I plant my foot upon this ground of trust and silence every man's fear with "God is just" to the needy. He is merciful and very caring. Some people will be crying when Jesus comes, while others will be rejoicing forever. People will be saying, "Lord, time has been very short!"

But I wonder who directs the Creator in His plans? My word to you is that you will be saved if you repent of your sins now and accept Jesus Christ as your savior. I believe that I will go to heaven by faith, and I will take my seat close to Jesus. Perhaps He will say to me, "Come, my son, for you served me in the world!"

This truth is found in the Bible. My heart is filled with great joy, and that's why I act after my call. That is why I am serving Him by reaching out to the needy and the hopeless. Jesus is coming to take me home. "He will send His angels with a great sound of a trumpet, and they will gather together His elect from the four winds, from one end of heaven to the other" (Matthew 24:31). That's why I am seeking the Lord in my life, as the Bible says: "For when they say, 'Peace and safety!', then sudden destruction comes" (1 Thessalonians 5:3).

Note that destruction comes when people are saying peace and safety. People today are focusing on peace and safety. We are entering a final chapter of human history. But to all those who have trusted Jesus Christ as their personal savior, they have confidence in their future because the Bible promises them a glimpse of heavenly bliss and eternal blessings that surpasses comprehension.

Some of the end-time prophesies are being fulfilled before our eyes. Wars, famines, earthquakes, natural disasters, and the critical world financial crises are affecting every nation on earth. Millions are dying today due to HIV/AIDS and other incurable diseases.

That's why I am telling you to accept Jesus Christ as your personal savior. The hour of this awful revelation is at hand. Surely, it is our time to seek the Lord! I want to work for God by serving others before it too late. God has given me a vision of reaching the unreached. I will focus on my dream. Through a dream, God saved the land of Egypt from the dangers of the famine.

That's why I am working hard to see my dream fulfilled. There is power in a dream. I have a dream of hope for Africa. One day I believe that God is going to set Africa free from tribal clashes, financial crises, calamities, disasters, floods, earthquakes, famines, and the HIV/AIDS pandemic.

I have a dream of a high level. The Bible says a dream can prevent people from perishing. My dream is a revelation of what the Lord is planning to do. It is God's will for His people. I have the real picture of what God wants to do in my ministry.

I know that God is going to bless Africa more than before. He is going to send us the greatest revival that the world has ever seen. God loves Africa. Africa belongs to Christ!

We are experiencing the greatest harvest of souls because the river of revival is flowing in Africa. Our churches and ministries will be revived in our midst as the Spirit of God moves.

Africa, I have a dream of hope for you. My dream is not going to tarry, and it will be fulfilled. People have been mocking me, calling me the "dreamer," but I have maintained my dream because I know it will come to pass!

God has a destiny for Africa. When God wants to bless people, He uses a dream or a vision. God starts with a dream. Africa will be blessed. The dream will not come to pass overnight, but I'm waiting for the dream to be fulfilled. God is very concerned with the needy and the hopeless people in Africa. That's why He is sending us to give the hopeless hope for survival.

God knows all your problems. He knows all the problems in Africa and in the whole world. Africa is walking to her destiny, and nobody, not even the devil, can stop us. God is changing Africa. He is our provider, a way maker where there is no way. He provides water in the desert.

God has opened doors for us in Africa. We are not going to perish. That is why we are hoping and trusting God in our lives. God is bringing us out soon!

Africa, walk to your destiny! Seek the Lord in righteousness and in holiness. Repent, Africa! This is the hour of your salvation, your deliverance, your visitation, your breakthrough, and your increase.

"Why are you cast down, O my soul? And why are you disquieted within me? Hope in God; For I shall yet praise Him, The help of my countenance and my God" (Psalm 42:11). In God, we have a brand-new hope. No one is hopeless whose hope is in God. Jesus said, "Because I live, you will also live" (John 14:19 NIV). I shall never lose hope, because I know that in Jesus Christ, survival is possible.

I am called to make a difference in this hurting world by reaching out to the needy in love. This is my ultimate dream, reaching the unreached and giving hope for survival to the hopeless. Jesus is able to see us through crises, disasters, tragedies, famines, floods, earthquakes, diseases, and turmoil. Jesus is our savior. Surely, He has borne our grief 's and carried our sorrows. He was wounded for our transgressions and bruised for our iniquities, and with His stripes, we are healed.

The Bible has a word of encouragement for the hopeless: "For you know the grace of our Lord Jesus Christ, that though He was rich, yet for your sakes He became poor, that you through His poverty might become rich" (2 Corinthians 8:9 NKJV). In Jesus Christ, there is survival for the hopeless in Africa. Never lose hope! You could be asking the question, "Is survival possible?" The answer is simple. With Jesus, our savior, survival is possible!

CHAPTER TWELVE

HOPE FOR SURVIVAL

The first atomic bomb in human history suddenly exploded over the Japanese town of Hiroshima, resulting in mass deaths and extensive damage that terrified mankind. Kenyans will never forget the July 8, 1998, bomb blast in Nairobi, which left many dead and others helpless with serious injuries.

Today everybody is living in fear due to terrorists, whose desire is to kill the Jews and everybody else who would support the Jews. In the book of Esther, the Bible describes the first attempt to destroy the Jews. Through the years, many such attempts have followed; for example, the Nazis in Europe. Hitler killed six million innocent Jews.

Today we have many groups in the Middle East against the Jews. I believe that the Jews are the chosen people of God. Regardless of the fact that they have rejected the one we accept as the Messiah, they are still God's people. We are praying for the Jews. We are aware that many who hate them are planning to destroy them again. I love the Jews, and I can say like Esther, "For how can I bear to see the calamity that is coming to my people? Or how can I bear to see the destruction of my kindred?" (Esther 8:6 ESV).

Esther stepped boldly into the presence of the king and made her plea on behalf of the Jews, God's chosen people. That saved the Jews, but even today, many are fighting to destroy the Jews and the Christians. Kenyans will never forget the two bomb blasts in Nairobi and Mombasa, which left many dead or badly injured and disabled. The media carried the terrorist attacks to the whole world. On television and in the papers, you could see the extent of this terrible scene.

You could see the fire, smoke, and dust in the air. High buildings fell and tumbled down onto the people who were walking on the streets. You could hear loud screaming, weeping, and cries from the victims who were agonizing in great pain and suffering. Flames and mountains of broken concrete covered some people. The rescue workers dug frantically to recover the bodies. The emergency workers and doctors were unable to handle the great number of causalities. Many people's hearts were horrified when they saw the victims lying in the street in intense pain.

The whole city was covered by a very heavy blanket of sorrow and death, which coiled around the city like a serpent. It was as if hell had opened its mouth wide to receive the victims. There was a cry of terror everywhere in the city. Many people were experiencing the deepest hell in their lives. To experience hell is to feel completely abandoned by the Living God. The area was in total terror.

People who worked in the offices watched helplessly as their friends lay dying. It was a terrible scene, and many people were overwhelmed with sorrow to the point of death. Others were crying hot and bitter tears of grief for their loved ones. This was a picture of hell on earth: "weeping and gnashing of teeth."

Some of the rural people in the upcountry were upset to the point of turning off their television sets. They did not want to see or hear this terrible news. They were looking to hear good news for a change. It seems that the power of evil has dominated our world today to the point where you can never hear good news. People are wondering whether this crooked generation will last. It is natural to have this kind of question because the world is full of wars, pains, troubles, and suffering. There is a fear in the hearts of human beings when evil things are unfolded before us daily. Everybody in Kenya was asking the question, "Why are the innocent attacked?"

This was the worst flow of shocking, depressing news we have ever had in our country. We are suffering because many people have gone astray; they are corrupt. There is no more who does good, not even one. These evildoers are eating the people of God as their bread, but the time is coming when they will face God's judgment. A time when they will be forever in hell in great terror and pain (Psalm 14:3–5). God is going to judge evildoers and sinners with justice.

When Cain killed his brother, Abel, God said, "What hast thou done? The voice of thy brother's blood crieth unto me from the ground. And now art thou cursed from the earth, which hath opened her mouth to receive thy brother's blood from thy hand" (Genesis 4:10–11 KJV).

Even today, the voice of the blood of the innocent people who died in the bomb blasts is crying from the ground. This picture of the people who were crying has remained in our minds since then.

Therefore, sin must not be treated lightly. Sin must be repented by all human beings in this world because it is causing untold troubles, pains, and suffering to many innocent people. Sin is a curse, which passed from one generation to another, so there nothing new under the sun.

Because of the curse, which Cain had received, his Son Lamech also killed a young man. He said, 'For I have slain a man to my wounding, and a young man to my hurt. If Cain shall be avenged sevenfold, truly Lamech seventy and seventy fold (Genesis 4:23–24).

"The wages of sins is death; but the gift of God is eternal life through Jesus Christ, our Lord" (Romans 6:23). In the world, we have millions of sad stories of victims of oppression and other evils who are crying to God for justice. If the terrorists remain unrepentant, they will receive an eternal judgment in hell for the destruction of the lives of innocent people. They will be punished together with unbelievers; idolaters, sexual perverts, liars, and criminals all will be in the fiery lake of burning sulfur forever and ever.

On September 11, 2001, America was suddenly attacked by terrorists who hijacked airplanes and crashed them into the World Trade Center, causing an explosion and fire, which left thousands dead and others severely wounded. The whole world lamented about this awful act of terror.

In the world today, there is a growing fear of what we call mass destruction by nuclear weapons, and the whole world is still talking about these awful tragedies which are caused by terrorists yet people fail to consider the horrifying fire and brimstone which is about to be revealed when the world comes to an end.

My friend, death is inevitable to all creation. So when it eventually knocks at your door, where will you spend eternity? "I'm tormented in this flame." This was the agonized cry of one who died, was buried, and awoke in the eternal world of the damned. I want you to focus on the second death, which will be eternal torment for some of us.

After reading the story of this man in the Bible, you probably might try to convince yourself that the second death, and your reckoning with God, is still a long way off.

In the story of the rich man and the poor man, Lazarus, the situation after death is clearly described. The rich man lived in sin, and after death, he went straight to hell. In hell, he lifted his eyes as he suffered pain, anguish, and torment. Poor Lazarus was righteous before God. After his death, his spirit went to Abraham's bosom, resting in paradise. But the rich man cried to God, "Have mercy on me and send Lazarus that he may dip the tip of his finger in water and cool my tongue...I'm tormented in this flame" (Luke 16:20–24).

My friend, you would better take note of this calamity and repent of your sins lest you end up in the lake of fire like the rich man. I am persuaded to think that this might be the last warning you will receive from God Almighty before He summons you into His presence. I pass on to you God's warning: "But the cowardly, unbelieving, abominable, murderers, sexually immoral, sorcerers, idolaters, and all liars shall have their part in the lake which burns with fire and brimstone, which is the second death" (Revelation 21:8 NKJV).

You might be living in sin like the rich man. You could be enjoying the pleasures of sin, but soon you might end up crying in hell with the rich man forever. "What is the use of gaining the whole world and losing eternal life?" ask yourself. "Treasures of the wickedness profit nothing: but righteousness delivereth from death [second death]" (Proverbs 10:2 KJV). The story of the rich man stirs my heart, and it constrains me to be more diligent in persuading men to repent. Don't be like the rich man who fooled himself by trying to seek salvation when he was surrounded by eternal fire. It was too late for him.

Millions are dying today, not knowing what the future holds for them. The time for your salvation is now! "As it is appointed unto men once to die, but after this the judgment" (Hebrews 9:27 KJV). Everything that you do is recorded in the books of God in heaven, and it will be revealed to you openly in the day of judgment (Revelation 20:12–14).

"Whosoever was not found written in the book of life was cast into the lake of fire" (Revelation 20:15). But why should you fear the second death when Jesus has shown you a clear way of escaping fire and brimstone. If fear grips your heart at this time, it is probably because you know deep within you that you have never honestly opened up your sinful life to Jesus Christ, Who is ready to cleanse you with His blood. So will you call on the merciful Savior right now?

The Bible has given you a chance to choose now where you will spend eternity. Remember that Jesus Christ is coming soon with your reward, which will be given according to your deeds. "He that is unjust, let him be unjust still: he which is filthy, let him be filthy still: and he that is righteous, let him be righteous still: and he that is holy, let him be holy still. And behold, I come quickly; and My reward is with Me, to give every man according as his work shall be" (Revelation 22:11–12).

The Blood of Jesus Christ, God's Son, Cleanses Us from All Sin (1 John 1:7)

Have you experienced this cleansing? Be honest, have you ever tried to walk in the light of God's presence in obedience to His word? Have you refused to accept the Savior due to preference for sin and pleasures, like the rich man? No wonder you will tremble before your creator at His judgment throne.

Even if your religion has been hypocritical of the Savior, to meet Him face-to-face is a must. There will be no foolish bravado and no cheering audience. Your little fear will be an unspeakable terror when you find yourself face-to-face with the holy God you have despised and mocked.

How often has He spoken to your heart, offering Himself as your savior, and you refused to listen? You prefer the sins that He hates. I would ask you to repent of your sins and avoid hell.

Why are you shutting your heart against the Savior's appeal? "Come unto me, all ye that labor [under the bondage of sin] and are heavy laden [under the guilt of sin], and I will give you rest" (Matthew 11:28) Yes, He is appealing to you now.

I prophesy to you now that when you least expect it, you will suddenly be in God's presence. A glance of faith at the Calvary marks on Jesus Christ's body will silence your every excuse. Your sin of refusing a free pardon at the cost of the Savior's blood will sink you into hell. The end is near; the Savior is pleading, and this may be the last plea! At this moment, there is hope for you, but after this...?

The Bible says that those who enter into the Lord's presence will find the fullness of joy and pleasures forevermore (Psalm 16:11).

My friend, I want to make you know that God is real, heaven is real, Satan is real, and hell is real. The day is surely coming when all unbelievers will wish they had never been born because they will die and wake up in hell where they will be in fiery torment like that man in the Bible. That day they will believe that hell is real, but it will be too late for them.

Sooner or later, you will face death. Everyone does. But Jesus Christ has already offered himself as a sacrifice for your sins. Accept his gift of salvation now, and you will avoid life's greatest disaster! There is hope for one like you; just believe in Jesus Christ. Never lose hope!

CHAPTER THIRTEEN

IN JESUS YOUR REDEMPTION IS ASSURED!

Almighty God has warned us in the Bible that the day of Christ's second coming will come as a thief who strikes in the night when no one is expecting it. He has graciously given us a number of signs to make us prepared for when it happens. The sudden destruction will occur when people are saying, "peace and safety." Notice that the focus of people's thoughts today is on peace and safety.

Let us think about the many peace movements that are spreading all over the world in which countless millions of terrified people, who know nothing of the inward peace of God in their hearts, are crying out for safety from nuclear destruction!

May I ask, "How can we expect to find peace and safety on earth while nuclear weapons are already aimed and located on vast areas for the destruction of the world at a moment's notice?" There is a growing fear in this world today for what is called the mass destruction by nuclear weapons.

Moreover, may I assure you that there is no promise in scripture of future time of peace and safety? Long ago, the

Bible revealed this truth: "There is no peace, saith the LORD, unto the wicked" (Isaiah 48:22).

So I honestly believe that there is no person or nation that will bring peace on earth when God has already declared war on a wicked and crooked generation. God, who lived in ancient history, is the same God who lives and reigns among the nations today. Therefore, do not be moved by the peace motions or false peace movements encircling the globe today. Rather be concerned that your godlessness and your immorality may provoke God to declare war on you directly. Who will save you then?

The false prophets would try hard to lure you into a false sense of security by promising you a glorious, peaceful, and prosperous life on earth, while the word of God says that this earth will melt with fervent heat. Let me assure you that there is no promise of a life of peace to sinners such as fornicators, adulterers, drug addicts, drunkards, and other sinners in the Bible. I stand to be corrected. If someone can show me such a scripture, I would be glad. The everlasting life of peace is for all those who are washed by the blood of Jesus Christ (Romans 5:1).

Jesus Is Coming

We are living in the end times when many people are perishing. In some nations of the world, people live in fear, turmoil, anxiety, depression, and suffering. These are the signs of the fulfillment of the words in the Bible, which says, "There shall be signs in the sun, in the moon and in the stars; and on the earth distress of nations, with perplexity; the sea and the waves roaring; men's hearts failing them from fear and the expectation of those things which are coming on the earth, for the powers of the heavens will be shaken. Then they will see the Son of Man coming in a cloud with power and great glory" (Luke 21:25–27 NKJV).

We are living in an hour unlike any other in the history of mankind when world leaders do not know the answer for the evil things which are happening in the world today. Our cities are plagued by an epidemic of violent crimes, and gangs of armed criminals are assaulting and robbing innocent people in their homes.

There is an increase of sexual insanity in our days when rapists are defiling women and girls, even those at a very young and tender age. Sexual immorality and sexual perversion are directly responsible for the spread of the HIV/AIDS epidemic that is killing millions in our modern world today. Families are perishing for lack of food, and others are filing for divorce.

Everywhere in the nation, people cry for help, and some are suffering from famines, floods, wars, tribal wars, and general conflict. These are the signs of the end times in a demon possessed society. A dispensation is passing away, and we are in the middle of the nightmare where the world is full of evil things, and man is rushing willingly into troubles. There is no peace in the air, in the sea, or in the land. Jesus is the only hope for this world. We are waiting for the dawning of this glorious day when suddenly Jesus, the Prince of Peace, the King of kings, shall appear in great glory in the clouds.

We are anxiously waiting for this glorious day, which will come very suddenly, for it will catch many sinners in their sin unprepared and unaware. The majority of people will be going on with their businesses as usual. The rich people will be gathering much wealth for themselves, and the poor will be caught complaining about their plight. Many people seek solutions for their problems, but there are no solutions without turning to Jesus for help!

Let me tell you plainly that the signs show us that Jesus is just about to come anytime, though we don't know the day. The Bible explains about this day in the parable of ten virgins: "At midnight a cry was heard: 'Behold the bridegroom, is coming; go out to meet him!'" (Matthew 25:6). In the world today, the spiritual atmosphere is changing, and we are expecting the Son of God anytime soon. Within us, we have a deep spiritual sense and consciousness that our redemption draws near.

There is a still voice saying, "Lift up your heads, because your redemption draws near" (Luke 21:28). Let us stop divisions, strife's, wrangles, and conflicts in the churches and win as many souls as possible into the kingdom. Jesus is coming soon—suddenly—and there will be no further notice. There will be no more time for us to be prepared.

My dear friend, we are entering a final chapter of human history, but all those who have trusted Jesus Christ as their personal savior have confidence in their future. For the Bible promises them a glimpse of heavenly bliss and eternal blessings that surpasses comprehension. A day is coming when the Lord will come to take us home because we are the chosen generation who will usher in the glorious coming of Jesus Christ. We are anxiously waiting for the trumpet of God, which will blast through the air as we prepare to meet our savior.

Some of the end-time prophesies are being fulfilled before us: wars, famines, earthquakes, natural disasters, and the critical world financial crisis affecting every nation on earth. Millions are dying today due to incurable diseases, wars, and starvation.

I would urge you to flee to Jesus and let Him save your life today. To a Christian, life is very promising because you shall live in a new world forever. This is a life of joy and fulfillment. The time for you to decide to trust in Jesus is now. There is no other opportunity after this.

To all those who do not believe in Jesus, life is not promising. The Bible says the wrath of God will be poured out on the earth; there will be incredible bloodshed, horror, and eternal death, forever.

Remember that the heavens and earth shall pass away in a flaming fire on the day of the Lord. And, suddenly, Christ will appear in the clouds. "In such an hour as ye think not, the Son of man cometh" (*Matthew 24:44 KJV*). For as the lightning cometh out of the east, and shineth even unto the west; so shall also the coming of the Son of man be" (*Matthew 24:27*). The hour of this awful revelation is at hand. Surely, it is time to seek the Lord. "For when you say, 'Peace and safety!'...sudden destruction comes" (*1 Thessalonians 5:3 NKJV*). Jesus is coming soon—suddenly.

Where are you spending eternity: in hell or heaven? I am a gospel messenger. I prophesy to you now that when you least expect it, you will suddenly be dashed into God's presence after your death. Your sins will sink you in the deepest hell.

The end is near. The Savior is pleading, and this may be your last chance. At this moment, there is hope for you. I'm living for Christ, and He is using me to reach the unreached. I'm serving as a herald of this wonderful wave of revival that is flowing in Africa today and I will never lose hope!

ABOUT THE BOOK

THE WORLD IS SITTING in the shadow of death due to the increase of conflicts, civil wars, crises, pandemics, threat of nuclear war and terror attacks. Where shall we get solutions for all these problems? As human beings created by God, we should be very careful not to lose hope of who we are and what we were created for. God wants to redeem you from your sins and use you to preach His redemptive love in this hurting world.

The author, Bishop Muya, has a very rich blend of biblical teachings, personal insights and heartfelt testimonies which has led many people to redemption after having a personal relationship with Jesus Christ. Your faith in Him can save you from earthly problems and eternal destruction.

Read this inspiring book, Hope For Survival, and you will discover that in Jesus Christ redemption is possible. When JESUS died for our sins, He was like a tree that was cut down, but it sprouted again. JESUS resurrected with a new life and His resurrection power brought new life into the deadness of the author's life because of his sins. Will you believe in Him now and you will receive eternal life?. "When they shall say, peace and safety, then sudden destruction comes upon them...and they shall not escape" [*1 Thessalonians 5.3*] With God everything is possible. There is Hope For Survival!

<u>ABOUT THE AUTHOR</u>

PETER. N. MUYA worked with Full Gospel Church and Redeemed Gospel Church, before starting his own ministry, Gospel Messengers Church. He was born in 1955 in Nyonjoro farm, Lanet, Nakuru County. He has a bachelor's degree in ministry, an associate's degree in biblical studies and counseling.

Other books by the author, the Gospel Messenger, Kill Me Not, Never Lose Hope, Do Not Weep, Love without Lust and I Shall Not Die.

He is married to Mary Muya, and they have three children who are adults working in different parts of our country. He is the founder and the Bishop of Gospel Messengers Church in East Africa.

Also by Peter N Muya

Kill Me Not

Love Without Lust

Do Not Weep

Death From Illicit Brew

I Shall Not Die

Never Lose Hope

About Us

Gospel Messengers Church is a nonprofit dedicated to transforming lives in Kenya's most marginalized communities. Committed to eradicating female genital mutilation (FGM), poverty, and illiteracy, the organization builds schools, provides clean water through boreholes, and empowers communities through education and sustainable development.

By addressing social injustices and uplifting vulnerable populations, Gospel Messengers Church fosters hope and opportunity for the less fortunate.

You can Donate via M-Pesa Pay Bill no: 89130 a/c: 110443.

You can also use PayPal email: messengergospel13@gmail.com

THESE ARE OUR BANK DETAILS FOR INTERNATIONAL MONEY TRANSFERS.

Bank Name	NCBA BANK KENYA PLC
Branch Name	NAKURU
Branch Code	000 (for any branch)
Bank Full Address	P.O. BOX 44599–00100, NAIROBI – KENYA
Bank Account Name	GOSPEL MESSENGER CHURCH
Bank Code	07
Bank Account Number	5146870014
SWIFT /BIC Code	CBAFKENX

www.ingramcontent.com/pod-product-compliance
Lightning Source LLC
Chambersburg PA
CBHW071339150726
47997CB00002B/794